# LOUISIANA

# LOUISIANA BY ROAD

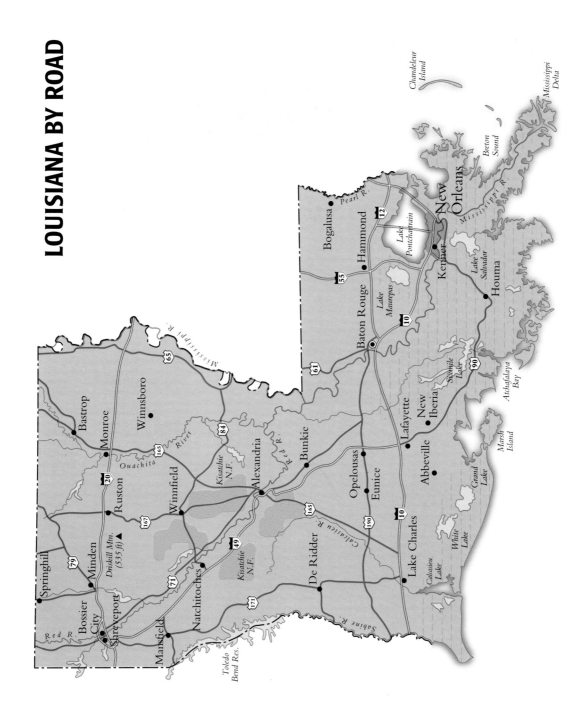

# CELEBRATE THE STATES
# LOUISIANA

## SUZANNE LeVERT

# BENCHMARK BOOKS

MARSHALL CAVENDISH
NEW YORK

*Dedicated to the warm and gracious people of Louisiana,
especially my friends Mary Ann Weilbaecher and Dan Fusillier.
With special thanks to Virginia Smith, Louisiana State Library*

Benchmark Books
Marshall Cavendish Corporation
99 White Plains Road
Tarrytown, New York 10591-9001

Library of Congress Cataloging-in-Publication Data
LeVert, Suzanne.
Louisiana / Suzanne LeVert.
p.  cm. — (Celebrate the states)
Includes biographical references and index.
Summary: Surveys the geography, history, people, and customs of the state of Louisiana.
ISBN 0-7614-0112-1
1. Louisiana—Juvenile literature. [1. Louisiana.] I. Title. II. Series.
F369.3L48  1997  976.3—dc20   96-26802  CIP  AC

Maps and graphics supplied by Oxford Cartographers, Oxford, England

Photo research by Matthew Dudley

Cover Photo: *The Image Bank*, Harald Sund

The photographs in this book are used by permission and through the courtesy of: *Louisiana Office of Tourism*:
6-7, 13, 16, 30, 63, 68-69, 74 (bottom), 98-99, 110, 116 (top and bottom), 117 (top and bottom).
*Photo Researchers, Inc.*: Eastcott-Momatuik, 10-11, 61, 136; Lawrence Migdale, 15; Dan Guravich, 19;
Porterfield/Chickering, 48-49; Andy Levin, 64; Garry D. McMicheal, 81; Jeff Greenberg dMRp, 102;
G. Holton, 103; Susan Leavines, 105; A. L. Parnes, 120; Van Bucher, 123; Mathias Oppersdorff, back cover.
*Peter Arnold, Inc.*: R. Andrew Odum, 21. *The Image Bank*: Walter Bibikow, 22; Peter E. Beney, 78; Lou Jones,
84-85; Grant Faint, 112; John Lewis Stage, 135. c *D. Donne Bryant/DDB Stock Photos*: 24, 74 (top), 82, 107,
108, 124. *From The Collection of the Louisiana State Museum*: 26-27, 35, 79. *Joslyn Art Museum, Omaha
Nebraska; Gift of the Enron Art Foundation*: 29. *The Historic New Orleans Collection*: (Acc. No. 1970.1) 31,
(Acc. No. 1953.107) 39, (Acc. No. 1974.25.9.290) 41, (Acc. No. 1974.25.25.113) 46. *Corbis-Bettmann*: 38,
127, 129 (top), 131. *UPI/Corbis-Bettmann*: 44, 53, 87, 88, 89, 94, 97, 128 (top and bottom), 129 (bottom),
133. *Reuters/Corbis-Bettmann*: 54, 126. *Springer/Corbis-Bettmann*: 92. *Courtesy The Mayor's Office of
Communications*: 57 (top and bottom). c *Jackson Hill/Southern Lights Photography*: 66. *Courtesy New Orleans
Historic Voodoo Museum*: 77.

Printed in Italy

3  5  6  4  2

# CONTENTS

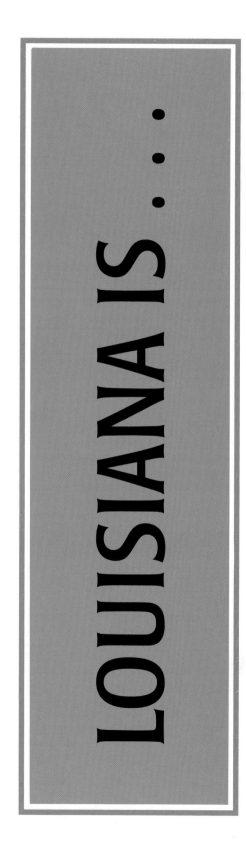

# LOUISIANA IS . . .

**Louisiana is steeped in spicy culture . . .**

"Laissez les bons temps rouler!" (Let the good times roll!)

—old French saying

"You come here and we say it's gonna be the blues, you know it's the blues, 'cause you gonna hear it, you gonna feel it."

—Tabby Thomas, blues artist and owner of the Blues Box and Heritage Hall in Baton Rouge

**. . . tinged with scandal . . .**

"The Devil has a very large empire here."

—French settler Le Père Antoine de Sedella, 1821

"I don't pretend to be honest. I only pretend to be as honest as anybody in politics . . . Why everybody is demoralized down here. Corruption is the fashion."

—Nineteenth-century Louisiana governor Henry Clay Warmoth

"Relax darlin'. This is the Big Easy. People have a certain way of doin' things down here."

—from *The Big Easy*, a 1986 movie about police corruption in New Orleans

**. . . and endowed with a strange and mysterious beauty.**

"This savage and deserted place, which the canebrake and trees cover almost entirely, will one day, and perhaps that day will not be distant, be a wealthy city and a metropolis of a great and rich culture." —Philippe, duc d'Orléans, seventeenth century

"To really understand, you have to nose a boat deep into the swamp on a summer evening and lie low until the snowy egrets fly into the roost and darkness swallows the cypress and tupelo trunks. You wait, and the swamp begins to speak. It croaks. It slurps, hoots, whistles, and shucks. It barks, chatters, hisses and cries; splashes, gurgles, and swallows."
— writer John Eastcott for *Audubon* magazine

**Most of all, Louisiana is full of warm people with big dreams.**

"I came here twenty-seven years ago from Mexico City, unable to speak English, and afraid. But the people here helped me, and I liked the spicy food and the music and the warm weather. Today, I have four sons, all going to college in Louisiana."
—Dario Rodriguez, New Orleans taxi cab driver

"Every Man a King."
—slogan from Huey Long's 1930 U.S. Senate campaign

In the pages that follow, you'll read about the unique and dynamic state of Louisiana, its colorful politics, its rich culture, its fascinating history, and, most important, its dynamic and dedicated citizens.

# 1 A SEMI-LIQUID PARADISE

**W**hile dinosaurs roamed the rest of North America some two hundred million years ago, water covered much of what is today Louisiana. During the Cenozoic Era, the most recent unit of geologic time, the waters receded, exposing the land. Water still covers much of the state today. "The shape of the place changes minute by minute as the tides ebb and flow," says Andy Fournet, a shrimper in the bayous of southern Louisiana. "I'm always noticing new inlets in some places and new land where there wasn't any before."

## PINE TREES AND MARSHLAND

All of Louisiana lies within the rich fertile Gulf Coastal Plain. Three distinct regions bring variety to this low-lying land: the East Gulf Coastal Plain, the Mississippi Flood Plain, and the West Gulf Coastal Plain.

The *East Gulf Coastal Plain* is a small portion of the state east of the Mississippi River. Here, rolling prairies in the north give way to southern marshland. The *Mississippi Flood Plain* straddles the Mississippi River from the Arkansas border to the Gulf of Mexico. Formed by silt brought down from the north by the Mississippi, this area contains the most fertile soil in the state. Both Baton Rouge, the state capital, and New Orleans, Louisiana's largest and most populated city, are found here. The plains and prairies of the

*The evening sun casts a glow over the Mississippi River, the centerpiece of Louisiana's economy and the heart of its landscape.*

*West Gulf Coastal Plain* fill the entire western half of the state. The state's highest peak, 535-foot Driskill Mountain, rises from the prairie just forty miles south of the Arkansas border.

The coastline of the Gulf of Mexico forms the region's southern border. Barrier beaches—ridges of sand formed by the tides—help protect the inner beaches from erosion.

## WATER, WATER, EVERYWHERE

"Ol' Man River, That Ol' Man River . . . He just keeps rollin' along."
"Ol' Man River," the song that Jerome Kern wrote for the musical
*Show Boat*, evokes the Mississippi River's enduring power. From
its source in northern Minnesota, America's most important water-
way wends its way south for more than 2,350 miles into Louisiana.
Along the way, it picks up millions of tons of sediment (sand and
soil), which it drops at the mouth of the Gulf of Mexico. The land
formed by this buildup, the Mississippi Delta, spreads across one-
fourth of the state.

Another liquid feature of Louisiana is the bayou. "A bayou is a
place that seems often unable to make up its mind whether to be
earth or water and so it compromises," writes historian Harnett
Kane. A geographical term unique to Louisiana, a bayou is a slow-
moving body of water that is connected to a lake, river, or sea. Many
freshwater bayous in Louisiana are actually former mouths of the
Mississippi River, which has changed its course countless times
throughout its long history. Overflow from the Gulf of Mexico has
created many salty bayous.

Louisiana's marshes, or wetlands, bring many important
resources to the state. Wetlands are stretches of treeless land in
which water lies above the surface of the ground. Unlike bayous,
wetlands may be unconnected to other bodies of water. Louisiana's
coastal wetlands represent nearly half of the nation's wetlands.
They support the largest fish and shellfish industry in the country
and create a home for millions of native and migratory birds.

Louisiana also has its share of impressive lakes. Lake Pontchartrain (PON-sha-trane), just north of New Orleans, sprawls over six

## THE CREATION OF BAYOU TECHE

The Bayou Teche (pronounced BI-yoo-tesh) is 125 miles of twisting and turning water that runs through the heart of Cajun country. The word Teche comes from the Native American word *tenche*, meaning "snake." According to legend, Indian warriors discovered a giant serpent. When they shot him full of arrows, he began to twist and writhe in pain. The dying snake, the legend goes, dug out the curvaceous bayou during his death struggle, and so left Louisiana with one of its life-giving waterways.

hundred square miles. The water is brackish, a combination of freshwater and saltwater. Other brackish lakes in Louisiana are Lake Maurepas and Lake Borgne. Most of the state's freshwater lakes, including Caddo Lake, Lake Bistineau, and Catahoula Lake, are found in the north.

*A cypress in Lake Palourde. "It ain't Spanish and it ain't moss," says a tour guide of the lacy foliage that drapes over most of Louisiana's oak and cypress trees. Spanish moss actually belongs to the pineapple family.*

As if all this inland water weren't enough, Louisiana's entire southern border stretches 397 miles along the Gulf. The fifth-largest body of water in the world, the Gulf of Mexico is one of the state's most important economic resources. Its warm waters hold abundant fish and shellfish, and oil and natural gas deposits lie deep within its seabed.

## A SUBTROPICAL PARADISE

It's hot, hot, hot—and when you're talking about Louisiana, you're not just talking about the spicy food or the foot-tapping jazz. You're talking about the temperature outside. During much of the year, Louisiana is very warm and humid. Temperatures hover in the nineties, and the air is often heavy with moisture. Even today, with almost every public building and private home equipped with air-conditioning, Louisianians struggle with the summer heat. "I think that's why things move more slowly in the South," says Johanna Weiss of Baton Rouge. "It's so sultry, no one expends more energy than necessary."

Heavy rainfall often beats down on this coastal state. On average, more than fifty-seven inches of rain fall every year. Even in the depths of winter, it rarely gets cold enough to snow. Some days in February can be as warm as days in August, but cold air can sweep in quickly from the north. The storm Native Americans named "huracan" is a constant threat to all the states that lie along the Gulf. A storm earns the name hurricane when winds reach a speed of seventy-four miles per hour or greater. Since 1875, about thirty hurricanes have ripped along the Louisiana coast. "I've been here

# LAND AND WATER

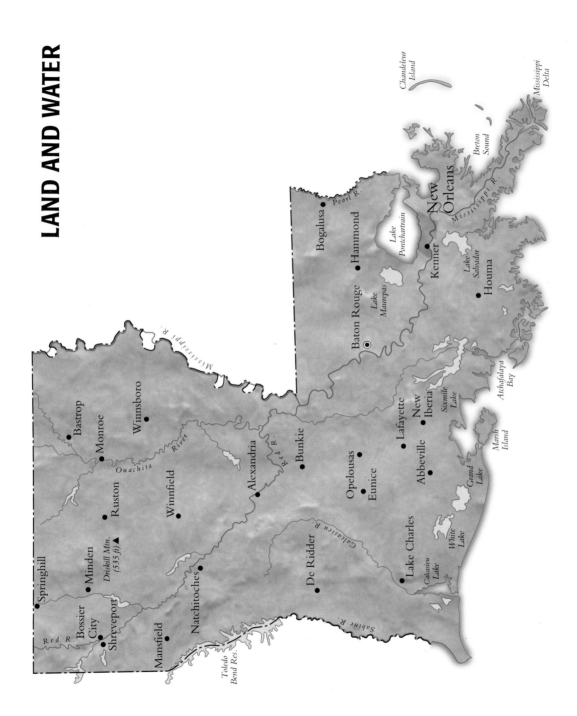

Chandeleur Island

Mississippi Delta

Breton Sound

Pearl R.

New Orleans

Bogalusa

Hammond

Lake Pontchartrain

Kenner

Lake Salvador

Baton Rouge

Lake Maurepas

Houma

Mississippi R.

Mississippi R.

Winnsboro

Bastrop

Monroe

River

Atchafalaya Bay

Ouachita

Lafayette

New Iberia

Sixmile Lake

Ruston

Winnfield

Alexandria

Red R.

Bunkie

Opelousas

Eunice

Abbeville

Marsh Island

Springhill

Minden

Driskill Mtn. (535 ft)▲

Grand Lake

Calcasieu R.

De Ridder

Lake Charles

White Lake

Bossier City

Shreveport

Natchitoches

Calcasieu Lake

Red R.

Mansfield

Sabine R.

Toledo Bend Res.

for a lot of the storms," boasts Marie Levert of Grand Isle. "It can get pretty wild when the winds whip up the sand and the rain comes so thick you can hardly see."

## THE WILD SIDE

Cypress trees dripping with Spanish moss . . . the scent of magnolias wafting in the breeze . . . the ungainly paddling of the brown pelican through a murky marsh . . . the buzzing of honeybees hovering over fragrant honeysuckle and hibiscus . . . The govern-

*The egret's brilliant white plumage is a frequent sight in the swamps and bayous of Louisiana.*

ment officials who picked Louisiana's state symbols—the bald cypress tree, magnolia blossom, brown pelican, and honeybee—chose well, especially considering how much they had to choose from. Louisiana's wildlife is as unique and varied as its landscape.

"Many people up north don't think of Louisiana as having forests," Peter Monroe of northern Louisiana remarks. "But I hunt deer in pine and oak forests up here all the time. And there are plenty of rabbits and raccoons, too."

Louisiana's swamps and marshlands are just as alive. In addition to harboring stands of oak and cypress trees, swamps teem with a variety of animals, birds, and fish. Human visitors to these watery habitats are sure to catch a glimpse of nutria (small beaver-like animals) paddling along and alligators sunning themselves on the shore. As peaceful as alligators might look in the sun, they can spring quickly into action. Wildlife photographer Julia Sims, who has seen many 'gators, says, "If you've ever heard an alligator bellow, you'd never forget it. The ground literally shakes beneath you." Graceful white herons and clumsy brown pelicans wade through the waters, during the winter sharing their home with 40 percent of all the migrating birds and ducks in North America.

Thanks to its subtropical climate, Louisiana stays in bloom throughout most of the year. The most abundant flower in Louisiana is the iris—and this slender flower comes in all colors here. Most irises grow in the rich bottomlands and marshes. Wild violets are almost as numerous, dotting the countryside with purple patches every spring. Fragrant magnolias, camellias, orchids, and azaleas bloom all over the state, from city gardens in New Orleans to wild meadows in the northwest.

# GHOSTLY 'GATORS

In 1987, a fisherman boating along a bayou in Terrebonne Parish came upon an awesome and mysterious sight: a pure white alligator. Although alligators have been on the planet for more than seventy million years, this was the first time a white alligator had ever been spotted. When scientists studied him and his all-white family, they discovered that they were missing a certain body chemical called melanin. Melanin gives alligator skin its brownish green color. Out of the more than one million alligators living in Louisiana's swamps, only about five hundred are all white.

As adults, alligators have no natural predators except humans, who have hunted alligators for their hides and meat for centuries. As infants, however, alligators have a number of natural enemies, including herons and turtles, who peck and snap them from the water with their sharp bills and teeth. In fact, scientists think that the reason there are so few white alligators is because they make such bright targets for these hungry predators!

## THE CITY LIFE

Until the 1940s, most Louisianians lived and worked on farms or in fishing villages. Today, Louisiana is almost completely "citified": More than two-thirds of its residents are clustered in urban areas. In fact, the state's three largest metropolitan areas—New Orleans, Baton Rouge, and Shreveport—are home to about half of Louisiana's total population. Most Louisianians live either in the north near the cities of Shreveport and Monroe, or in the southeastern part of the state, around New Orleans and Baton Rouge.

*The skyline of New Orleans sparkles over the Mississippi at night. "New Orleans is the greatest city in the world," proclaims native Harry Connick Jr., one of the city's most popular homegrown entertainers.*

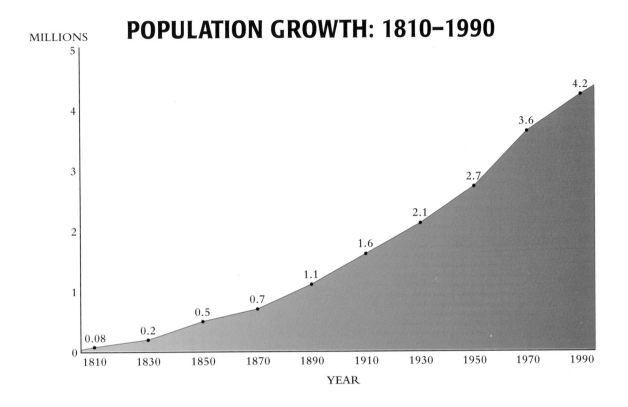

## POPULATION GROWTH: 1810–1990

MILLIONS

YEAR

About 4,360,000 people now call Louisiana home, making it the twenty-first most populous state in the nation. From the 1960s to the early 1980s, the booming oil and gas industries lured job seekers from all over the country. Since the decline of these industries, the state has experienced very slow growth.

## PROTECTING THE ENVIRONMENT

Like many other states, Louisiana has paid a very high price for its economic growth. Its highest-earning industries are also among the

*Pollution remains one of Louisiana's most pressing challenges. "It's a shame, that's what it is," says school-teacher Marie Charbeaux. "I know the economy depends on it, but the petrochemical plants are slowly killing everything that makes Louisiana so special—its bayous and wetlands and its wildlife. Even our state bird, the brown pelican, is in danger of dying off."*

greatest polluters in the nation, and its wetlands are being destroyed at an alarming rate.

**Pollution in the Pelican State.** "The old deal was a deal with the Devil—you send us the jobs and you can foul the air and the water," Representative Charles "Buddy" Roemer said in the late 1980s. Indeed, the petrochemical industries have wreaked havoc with Louisiana's land and water. In the early 1990s, the state ranked first in the nation in the amount of toxic waste in its waters and third in the amount of hazardous wastes it put into the ground. Only oil-rich Texas released more toxic gases into the air.

The Louisiana State Department of Environmental Quality has

been working hard to reverse those statistics. Since 1987, tougher laws have forced industries to reduce their chemical releases nearly 40 percent. The people of Louisiana help to clean up the environment, too. Recycling programs are in effect throughout the state, and an anti-littering campaign along the coast netted some 105,000 pounds of refuse that would otherwise have fouled wetlands and beaches.

**Shoring Up the Wetlands.** More than just beautiful scenery, the Louisiana wetlands are an invaluable economic and ecological resource for the whole country. Unfortunately, more than forty square miles of marsh sink beneath the water every year. One reason is a natural occurrence called subsidence: Sediment brought by the Mississippi tends to subside, or sink, under its own weight. Today, however, dams and levees along the Mississippi keep the river from bringing new sediment to the marshes when it floods in the spring. Another problem is that frequent storms erode barrier beaches which separate the marshes from the Gulf of Mexico. Finally, gas and oil drilling beneath the wetlands causes subsidence to occur at a much greater rate than is natural.

Scientists and ecologists continue to search for ways to protect the wetlands. One solution involves directing new offshoots of the Mississippi back into the marshes without posing a risk to nearby communities. Another way is to restore the barrier islands by building dikes to prevent them from washing away.

Louisianians are striving to improve their environment, but much work still needs to be done. It will take many more years and millions of dollars to restore the natural beauty lost in the name of progress.

# 2 RISE OF THE PELICAN STATE

Louisiana Landscape, by J. R. Meeker

Long before Europeans arrived on this continent, thousands of Native Americans lived on the land now known as Louisiana. The largest tribe of Louisiana natives, the Caddo, lived in the northwestern part of the state. A peace-loving tribe, the Caddo planted vegetables and hunted game. They lived in small villages with thatch-roofed timber houses. The Natchez lived in the north central part of the state, the Houma hunted and fished along the east bank of the Mississippi, and the Chitimacha lived west of the Mississippi. The Choctaw moved into Louisiana during the eighteenth century when British colonists forced them out of other parts of the southeast. The Choctaw soon became the largest tribe in Louisiana.

European expansion destroyed most of the Native American civilizations in Louisiana. Diseases like smallpox and measles brought by white settlers killed many natives, while settlers forced others out of their homelands to reservations in other parts of the country. Only one significant battle between whites and natives broke out in Louisiana. During the Natchez revolt in 1729, the Natchez tribe fought bravely but in vain against a group of European settlers. Later, in 1835, the last remaining tribe in Louisiana—the Caddo—ceded their land to the United States for $80,000.

*Choctaw Camp on the Mississippi, by Karl Bodmer. The Choctaw began arriving in Louisiana from the east in the 1760s. They settled along the west bank of the Mississippi, where they hunted and often sold game to neighboring farmers.*

## THE EUROPEANS ARRIVE

Explorers from Spain in search of gold were probably the first white people to catch sight of the Louisiana shore. In 1519, Alonso Alvarez de Piñeda came close to the Louisiana coast while navigating the Gulf of Mexico. About twenty-two years later, Hernando de Soto arrived by a different route. He and his men trekked overland across Florida, then sailed down the Mississippi River almost

# THE MYSTERIOUS MOUNDS AT POVERTY POINT

A spectacular seventy-foot-high sculpture of a bird rises from the earth. Next to it lies a huge octagon made up of several earthen mounds. This site, called Poverty Point, is one of the earliest and largest prehistoric settlements in North America.

The people of Poverty Point inhabited northeastern Louisiana between 1700 and 700 B.C. and established a highly developed culture. Archaeologists believe that the massive earthworks took some five million hours to build, a feat on the scale of the Great Pyramid of Egypt. The Poverty Point community also developed a remarkable trade network. They made stone tools from raw materials they found in the Ohio and Tennessee River valleys. Stone tools with serrated edges are unique to the Poverty Point culture.

In 1962, the U.S. Department of the Interior designated Poverty Point as a National Monument.

to its mouth. Since de Soto found no gold, though, the Spanish decided not to stay.

More than a century later, in 1682, French explorer René-Robert Cavelier, sieur de La Salle, sailed down the Mississippi and claimed all the surrounding land—the central third of the present-day United States—for France. He named this vast region Louisiana after King Louis XIV. For more than one hundred years, France and Spain passed this territory back and forth.

*On April 9, 1682, René-Robert Cavelier, sieur de La Salle, laid claim to the territory of Louisiana for King Louis the XIV of France. A great explorer known to be "a stern commander," La Salle was murdered by his own men only five years later.*

The French established their first settlement in Natchitoches (pronounced NAK-i-tish) in 1686, but found it difficult to attract settlers to this untamed and isolated part of the New World. King Louis XIV asked an organization of traders called the Company of the West to manage the colony. Headed by John Law, the Company tried several different schemes to attract settlers. Law distributed leaflets claiming that Louisiana was a "land filled with gold, silver, copper and lead mines"—an outright lie that lured fortune seekers by the hundreds to this uncharted land. With Law's encouragement, the French government allowed prisoners and debtors to pay for their crimes by moving to the new colony.

Nevertheless, not many people came to Louisiana until 1718. That year, Jean-Baptiste Le Moyne, sieur de Bienville, established a port city, which he called New Orleans. Located just 110 miles upstream from the mouth of the Mississippi River, New Orleans later became the commercial center of the South and one of the country's most important international ports.

Very quickly, the capital of the territory developed a character all its own. European settlers brought with them fine clothing and furnishings and established elegant traditions like banquets and balls. New Orleans also developed a reputation as a "city of sin." Music halls, bordellos, and gambling houses opened along the riverfront, and some former prisoners and ne'er-do-wells established a network of vice.

Physically, the city could be an extremely unpleasant place. Lying five feet below sea level along the river, New Orleans swarmed with mosquitoes and other insects. Deadly yellow fever epidemics were common. The heat and humidity were extreme. Frequent flooding turned streets into a sea of mud, and no sewer system existed to handle waste.

## THE SPANISH PERIOD

By 1762, France was deep in a costly war with Britain over control of North America. No longer able to afford to develop Louisiana, France offered the territory to Spain. For forty years, Spain helped Louisiana to flourish and added its special flavor to its heritage. When fire ravaged New Orleans in 1788, for instance, Spanish architects built a new city in the Spanish style, with elegant, cast-iron grillwork adorning the balconies.

The territory's population boomed at this time. New arrivals from Europe joined the original French and Spanish settlers, called Creoles. Germans established towns and villages in the north central region of the state. Scots, Irish, and British settlers arrived to settle in Louisiana's northeast. In 1763, several hundred Acadians established farms along the bayous west of New Orleans. Acadians were French settlers forced to leave Canada by the British during the Seven Years War. Some returned to France or went to other colonies, but many chose to settle in southern Louisiana, where they became known as Cajuns.

Slaves brought to work on Louisiana's expanding network of plantations made up the largest group of new residents. Many slaves were brought to the colony directly from the African regions of Guinea, the Gold Coast, and Angola. Others were taken from French islands in the Caribbean. By the beginning of the 1800s, more than thirty thousand slaves would live in Louisiana, making up nearly half of its population. Later, the moral and political consequences of slavery would nearly destroy the state and the country.

In the meantime, Louisiana played an important role in the American Revolution between Britain and its North American colonies. Spain, a long-standing rival of Britain, welcomed the revolution because it had the potential of weakening Britain. For almost four years, Spain secretly furnished colonists with supplies and weapons. American rebels and Spaniards often met in New Orleans because of the city's key location at the mouth of the Mississippi.

In 1800, after the defeat of the British in the American Revolution, Napoleon Bonaparte, emperor of France, pressured Spain into returning the territory to France. Once again—but only for a short time—the French flag flew over the land.

## BECOMING AMERICANS

In 1803, the French needed ready cash to finance another war with Britain. In a landmark deal that would almost double the size of the United States, President Thomas Jefferson bought the Louisiana Territory from France for only $15 million. A year later, Congress divided the territory into smaller, more manageable regions and named what would later become the state of Louisiana the Territory of Orléans.

When the people of Orléans applied for statehood in 1811, they caused a storm of protest in Congress. Some members saw Louisiana's culture as far more French than American, and the

*The Battle of New Orleans pitted six thousand British soldiers against a mere three thousand Americans. "By the Eternal," Andrew Jackson bellowed at his men about the invading British troops, "they shall not sleep on our soil." The Americans fought long and hard for several days until they finally emerged victorious.*

territory still had a reputation for lawlessness and loose living. Despite the controversy, on April 30, 1812, Louisiana became the eighteenth state to join the Union.

Just when Louisiana became a state, Britain and the United States became embroiled in another military struggle over territory called the War of 1812. Between December 1814, and January 1815, the British tried to capture the port of New Orleans. U.S. General Andrew Jackson drew together an unusual force. In addition to the

# THE BATTLE OF NEW ORLEANS

The Treaty of Ghent, ending hostilities between Britain and the United States in the War of 1812, was signed on December 24, 1814. American forces under the command of Major General Andrew Jackson soundly defeated the British in the Battle of New Orleans some two weeks later, on January 8, 1815. Neither army had received news of the treaty at the time of the battle.

'Twas on the eighth of— Jan - u - a - ry, just at the dawn of day, We spied those Brit - ish— of - fi - cers All— dressed in bat'le ar - ray. Old Jack - son then gave— or - ders: Each man to keep his post, And form a line from— right to left, And— let no time be lost.

regular militia, he enlisted Choctaws, and even a pirate named Jean Lafitte. On January 8, 1815, Jackson and his troops defeated the British in the Battle of New Orleans. Though the battle was fought after the war was officially over, the victory gave Louisianians a sense of pride in being American.

## THE AGE OF PROSPERITY

Cotton, sugar, and rice were the three most valuable crops in the world during the nineteenth century, and Louisiana's humid climate and rich soil were perfect for growing all three. More than 1,600 plantations—large farms where slaves worked the land and white owners lived in elegant mansions—dotted the state.

On January 10, 1812, the first steam-powered vessel puffed its way down the Mississippi River all the way from Pittsburgh, Pennsylvania, to New Orleans. Goods produced throughout the United States could now travel by river to the Gulf of Mexico and from there sail to international ports. Louisiana could also ship its own vast quantities of cotton, sugar, and rice into America's heartland.

By the mid-nineteenth century, Louisiana was no longer the isolated wilderness Hernando de Soto had discovered in 1541. New Orleans was the largest city in the South, the third largest city in the nation, and one of the busiest ports in the world. More than seven hundred thousand people lived in Louisiana in 1860 compared to just eighty thousand when it became a state.

But Louisiana's prosperity came at too high a price. For decades, the issue of slavery had divided the United States. Most Republicans, who favored abolishing (or ending) slavery, lived in the

## JEAN LAFITTE: PIRATE OR PATRIOT?

In 1806, the Territory of Orléans welcomed a new resident—the educated, charming, and dashingly handsome Jean Lafitte. Lafitte was no ordinary citizen: He was the chief of a band of outlaws. With headquarters on Barataria Bay in the Gulf of Mexico, Lafitte raided ships and smuggled slaves. At the same time, though, Lafitte remained a loyal patriot—at least in his own eyes and in the eyes of many of his compatriots. When an English captain offered him money to attack New Orleans during the War of 1812, Lafitte

refused. He then helped General Andrew Jackson win the Battle of New Orleans. Later, U.S. President James Madison pardoned Lafitte and his men for their acts of piracy as thanks for their service to the United States. Today, Louisianians are split in their opinions about their infamous son: Some consider Lafitte a pirate, others a patriot.

North, while most proslavery Democrats lived in the South. Tension reached a boiling point in November 1860, when confirmed antislavery candidate Abraham Lincoln was elected president of the United States.

## THE CIVIL WAR IN LOUISIANA

In February 1861, shortly after Lincoln became president, eleven southern states formed a new country called the Confederate States of America. Its first act was to declare war on the remaining states, known as the Union. The Civil War that followed would be a devastating and bloody affair for the entire nation.

Not everyone in Louisiana wanted to go to war. Many poor whites who did not own slaves refused to fight over the issue. Businessmen in New Orleans and Baton Rouge wanted to keep their trading partners in the north. Nevertheless, Louisiana joined the Confederacy and would fight long and hard for its losing cause.

*By the mid-nineteenth century, the Mississippi River town of New Orleans had become the largest port in the south, attracting goods and immigrants from all over the world.*

On December 3, 1861, Union troops landed on Ship Island. The war had come to Louisiana. Union ships led by Commodore David Farragut blocked the mouth of the Mississippi in April 1862 and most of the ports along the Gulf. The blockade cut off the flow of supplies to both Confederate troops and civilians. Union control over most of Louisiana lasted until the end of the war in 1865.

Two major Civil War battles took place on Louisiana soil. In May 1863, forty thousand Union troops led by General Nathaniel P. Banks tried to capture the capital city of Baton Rouge by attacking its fort, Port Hudson. Confederate troops under General Franklin Gardner fought bravely through a six-week siege, but finally surrendered. The Union flag was raised over Baton Rouge.

Now only northwestern Louisiana remained in Confederate hands. In April 1864, the Confederates won the bloody Battle of Mansfield. It was the final battle in the state and the last Confederate victory of the war. Their victory was a hollow one, however. As the Union troops withdrew, they destroyed property, crops, and livestock along the way. Within a year, General Robert E. Lee had surrendered at Appomattox, and the Confederate cause was lost.

## THE PAIN OF RECONSTRUCTION

The Civil War devastated Louisiana. The state's banking system had been ruined and one-half of its livestock had disappeared. Plantations lacked the slave labor needed to cultivate crops. Worst of all, some twelve thousand young men were killed by bullets or disease, and many more were disabled.

The South's whole world turned upside down after its defeat.

*The bloody Battle of Mansfield saw Confederates charging forward like "infuriated demons" to vanquish the Union forces. This was the last Confederate victory of the Civil War.*

Slaves were freed and given the right to vote and hold office. The Democratic Party, once in control, now had to bow to Republican interests. In order to be admitted back into the United States, Louisiana had to allow federal officials to oversee elections. Backed by armed troops, these officials registered black voters and denied the vote to any white who had aided the Confederacy.

Federal control over Louisiana's internal affairs—called Reconstruction—lasted about ten years. Although the aims of Reconstruction were admirable, the methods employed by many Republican officials were both ruthless and corrupt. Soliciting bribes, embezzling state funds, and rigging elections were common practices.

Humiliated and anxious to regain power, white Democrats of Louisiana formed secret antiblack militias like the White League and the Ku Klux Klan. These groups terrorized blacks and any whites who supported the Democrats. In 1874, members of the White League lynched six Republicans at Coushatta in northwest Louisiana. Two weeks later, the White League overpowered the Metropolitan Police in the Battle of Liberty Place in New Orleans. A few years later, Reconstruction was over.

## THE BOURBON ERA

From the end of Reconstruction in 1877 until the 1920s, power remained in the hands of a small group of wealthy men known as the Bourbon Democrats. The Bourbons believed that government should not play a large role in the lives of its citizens. The Bourbons also promoted the idea that white people were better than black people and should have more power and money. Because federal law gave African Americans the right to participate in the political process, the Bourbons used fear and intimidation to keep blacks from gaining power within the state. Vigilante groups like the Ku Klux Klan and the White League thrived, especially in the northern part of the state.

Under the Bourbons, the majority of Louisianians sank deeper into poverty. Modern industry came more slowly to Louisiana than it did to the rest of the country. The government did not pay very much to improve schools, to build roads, or to maintain other public services. The state remained in the grip of racism and poverty throughout the first two decades of the twentieth century.

## THE LONG EMPIRE

On August 30, 1893, a boy named Huey Pierce Long Jr. was born in Winn Parish, Louisiana. As a child, Long heard a lot of political talk about Populism, a political movement that sought to unite poor whites and poor blacks against the wealthy few who held all the power. He also grew up seeing how poor people in Louisiana lived. School children had no books to study, farmers couldn't get to market because no roads existed or the ones that did were muddy and rutted.

Long was an extremely ambitious man. Although he dropped out of high school, he managed to get through law school at Tulane University before turning to politics. Huey Long launched his first race for governor in 1924, but lost. Four years later, he promised the people of Louisiana better schools and roads and said he would support poor farmers against the powerful oil, railroad, and electric corporations. The people of Louisiana, anxious to improve their lot, voted him into office.

As governor, Long accomplished many of his goals. But he did resort to ruthless and power-hungry methods. He forced legislators to vote for his bills, took in and spent money freely, and ignored the law when it kept him from doing what he wanted. When chal-

*"There may be smarter men than me, but they ain't in Louisiana," said Huey Pierce Long, the state's most dynamic and often ruthless governor. Long is pictured here with his son Russell, who would serve as Louisiana's U.S. Senator for more than thirty-seven years.*

lenged by a legislator who held up the state constitution, Huey Long simply said, "I am the Constitution here." At one point during his term, the legislature nearly impeached Long.

At the same time, though, the state and the nation as a whole were sinking into the Great Depression. More than 15 percent of the state's population went on relief. The people of Louisiana wanted Huey Long in office because he made them believe that things would get better. He increased funding for education and provided free textbooks for all schoolchildren. He began construction of roads and bridges throughout the state.

In 1930, Long won a seat in the U.S. Senate, although he did not give up his position as governor until 1932. He then made plans to run for president. Just as his campaign was gaining momentum, the son of one of his political enemies shot him to death in the Louisiana state capitol. The year was 1935. Although Huey's own flamboyant career ended in assassination, the state continues to feel his influence. Other members of the Long family made their marks on Louisiana, too. Huey's brother Earl served three terms as governor in the 1940s and 1950s—and stirred up almost as much controversy as Huey himself. Huey's son Russell served in the U.S. Senate from 1948 to 1969.

## INTO MODERN TIMES

Back in 1901, when Huey Long was just eight years old, a prospector drilled Louisiana's first oil well in a small bayou town named Jennings. For the next several decades, prospectors would mine more and more oil, gas, and chemicals from the earth. Forever after, the petrochemical industry would form the heart of the Louisiana economy.

Louisiana did not emerge from the Great Depression until the U.S. involvement in World War II sparked its economy. Jobs became plentiful when the government began tapping oil, petroleum, and other industries to provide supplies. One company, the Higgins Shipyard of New Orleans, led the nation in the production of small naval craft, and the number of manufacturing jobs in Louisiana doubled between 1940 and 1950.

The social texture of Louisiana also began to change. People left

*The fight for civil rights was hard fought in Louisiana. Here, white citizens have taken to the streets in protest of desegregation of the state's public schools. It wasn't until November 1961 that the first four black children entered a formerly all-white school in New Orleans, thereby ending official segregation in the state.*

their farms and fishing villages for New Orleans, Baton Rouge, and other big cities. Slowly, Louisiana took its first steps toward integration. In 1960, four black children became the first in the state to go to once all white schools in New Orleans. White parents held a huge rally against integration, and violence erupted. It would be many years before race relations improved. In 1977, the people of

New Orleans took a big step forward by electing a black man, Ernest "Dutch" Morial, as their mayor, and today hundreds of African Americans serve in public office.

During the 1970s, Louisiana experienced its biggest economic boom ever when international oil prices skyrocketed. New roads and highways were built, the education budget was increased, and health care was vastly improved. Then, just as suddenly, in 1983 prices on the world oil market plummeted. Louisiana's economy nearly collapsed. By 1986, it had an unemployment rate of 13 percent, the highest in the nation.

Since that time, the people of Louisiana have been working together to improve their quality of life. As they head for the twenty-first century, they have many challenges to meet, but also much to celebrate.

# 3 FACING GREAT CHALLENGES

*The state capitol in Baton Rouge.*

**D**espite its rich natural resources and physical beauty, Louisiana is one of the nation's poorest states and has among the highest rates of crime, unemployment, adult illiteracy, and infant mortality. Luckily, the people of Louisiana are tenacious—they have the will to make things better for themselves and their children. They also possess a certain "joie de vivre" (joy of living) that makes even these tough challenges seem possible to meet.

## INSIDE GOVERNMENT

From the start, Louisianians have been fussing with the makeup of their government and the laws of their state. In fact, Louisiana has had eleven different constitutions, more than any other U.S. state. The present constitution was enacted in 1975.

This constitution contains a remarkable bill of rights, one of the most progressive in the country. "No law shall discriminate against a person because of race or religious ideas, beliefs, or affiliations," the bill states. "No law shall arbitrarily, capriciously, or unreasonably discriminate against a person because of birth, age, sex, culture, physical condition, or political ideas or affiliations." This addition to the state constitution shows how far Louisiana has come since its 1868 constitution, which essentially denied all but white men with property the right to vote.

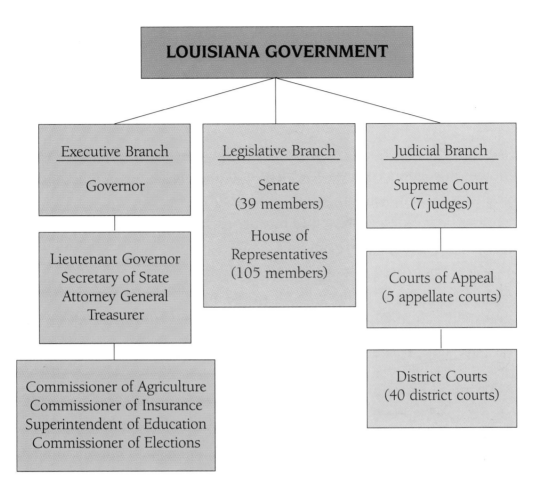

**LOUISIANA GOVERNMENT**

**Executive Branch**

Governor

Lieutenant Governor
Secretary of State
Attorney General
Treasurer

Commissioner of Agriculture
Commissioner of Insurance
Superintendent of Education
Commissioner of Elections

**Legislative Branch**

Senate
(39 members)

House of
Representatives
(105 members)

**Judicial Branch**

Supreme Court
(7 judges)

Courts of Appeal
(5 appellate courts)

District Courts
(40 district courts)

"Politics in Louisiana are almost as popular as football in Indiana," remarks Dan Fournier, a native of the state. Indeed, Louisiana's politics have always been spirited and exciting. Its elected and appointed officials work in three different branches: the executive, legislative, and judicial.

**Executive.** The head of Louisiana's executive branch is the governor, who is elected to a four-year term. By law, a Louisiana governor cannot serve more than two consecutive terms but can serve an unlimited number of terms. The governor of Louisiana has many powers and duties; they include appointing judges and certain other officials, preparing the state budget, and considering proposed laws for enactment.

The office of governor is a powerful position, which many ambitious, talented, and colorful men have held. Some have used their power for good, others for personal or political gain. Henry Warmoth, who served from 1868 to 1872, was called "the shrewdest, boldest, ablest, and most conscienceless young man" by his former commanding officer, Ulysses S. Grant.

After his brother Huey's assassination, Earl Long served three nonconsecutive terms as governor (and was elected a fourth time but died before taking office), despite a great deal of controversy surrounding his personal and political life. Governor John J. McKeithen led his state through the difficult process of integration while expanding its economy during his two consecutive terms, from 1964 to 1972.

Edwin W. Edwards served the most time as governor—two consecutive terms from 1972 to 1980, then again from 1984 to 1988 and from 1992 to 1996. Edwards was the state's first governor of Cajun heritage. He helped move Louisiana forward during its economic boom time during the 1970s. He, too, stirred up his share of controversy. A notorious gambler, Edwards once told a reporter that he kept $800,000 in ready cash for his trips to Las Vegas. In 1985, he was indicted (but never convicted) on federal racketeering charges. And still the people of Louisiana wanted him to govern. J. Bennett Johnston, an associate, once said of him: "Edwin's greatest strength and his greatest weakness is his ability to

*Like his older brother Huey, Louisiana governor Earl Long appealed to the poor and working class. "We got the finest roads, finest hospitals, finest schools in the country," Earl Long bragged during a campaign speech, "yet there are rich men who complain [about taxes]. They are so tight, you can hear 'em squeak when they walk."*

come within a millimeter of the law without breaking it." Edwards won an unprecedented fourth term in 1992, but decided not to run again in 1996.

Mike Foster, a conservative Republican, followed Edwards into the governor's office. Foster's very first action as governor stirred up a hornet's nest of controversy. He eliminated the state's affirmative action programs designed to give African Americans and other minorities a better chance to compete in business. He

# 1992: A STORM OF CONTROVERSY

"Vote for the Crook—It's Important."

So read a popular bumper sticker in support of Edwin Edwards during the 1992 campaign for Louisiana governor, one of the most controversial elections in the state's colorful history. David Duke, a former high-ranking member of a racist organization, was pitted against incumbent governor Edwin Edwards, a gambler once indicted for racketeering, or obtaining money from illegal activities.

The election highlighted Louisiana's traditional political divisions. Duke attracted many of the white, lower-income Baptists living primarily in the northern part of the state, while Edwards received votes from nearly all the blacks in the state and about 50 percent of white votes. Most whites who voted for Edwards were Catholic, relatively wealthy, and living in the south. In fact, were it not for the fact that 96 percent of all Louisiana's blacks—who make up more than 30 percent of the state's population—voted for Edwards, Louisiana might have elected a known racist to its highest state office.

Edwin Edwards won the election and served out his fourth and final term as governor. The 1992 campaign appears to have been David Duke's final moment of fame. After losing the election, he turned to selling insurance in Metairie, a city on the outskirts of New Orleans.

claimed that these programs were no longer necessary and that employment should be based solely on merit.

**Legislative.** Louisiana's citizens elect members to two houses of the state legislature: 39 members to the Senate and 105 members to the House of Representatives. Both senators and representatives serve four-year terms. These men and women work together to create laws. When both the Senate and the House agree upon a proposed law—called a bill—the legislature sends it to the governor. If the governor signs it, the bill becomes law. If the governor vetoes (rejects) the bill, it goes back to the legislature. If two-thirds of both houses still want the bill to become law, they can vote to override the veto.

**Judicial.** Louisiana's highest court is the supreme court, which has a chief justice and six associate justices, all elected to ten-year terms. The court system also includes five courts of appeal and forty district courts.

Louisiana's legal system is based on what is known as civil law. Civil law is based on the Napoleonic code of France—a vestige of Louisiana's French past. Under civil law, judges decide cases on the basis of a written set of rules. They can disregard decisions made by other judges about similar cases. Other states practice common law, which bases its rulings on previous court decisions, also called precedents.

## MAYORS AND MANAGERS

Louisiana is divided into sixty-four units of local government called parishes. The term comes from the days of French and Spanish rule when the Catholic Church dubbed its districts parishes. Today many parishes are governed by a body called a police jury, which acts much like a town council.

New Orleans and other large cities, like Shreveport and Monroe, have mayors as their chief executives. New Orleans is the largest, wealthiest, and most populated city in the state. Like Louisiana as a whole, New Orleans faces some big challenges. Its crime rate was the highest in the nation in 1994, and more people moved out of the city than moved in.

The mayor of New Orleans in 1996 was Marc Morial, the son of the much beloved Ernest "Dutch" Morial, the city's first black mayor. *New Orleans* magazine described Marc Morial as "a young, hopeful mayor in a big, problem-ridden city."

Together, the state and local governments work on behalf of the people of Louisiana. Their goal is to make the state a healthy place in which to live, learn, grow, and work.

## LOUISIANA WORKING . . .

"The Big Easy"—that's one of Louisiana's nicknames, and a well-deserved one at that. Both the weather and the people are warm, and it's easy to imagine whiling away the hours sitting alongside a meandering bayou or chatting away with friends in a New Orleans café.

But the living in Louisiana is not always so easy. More people live in poverty here than anywhere else in the nation except the District of Columbia. The average income of Louisianians is 20 percent lower than that of most other Americans.

In 1978, Ernest "Dutch" Morial became the first black mayor in New Orleans' history by developing a reputation as a "rigidly honest, and non-militant" civil rights leader.

Marc Morial, son of Dutch Morial, took the helm as mayor of New Orleans in 1996.

# EARNING A LIVING

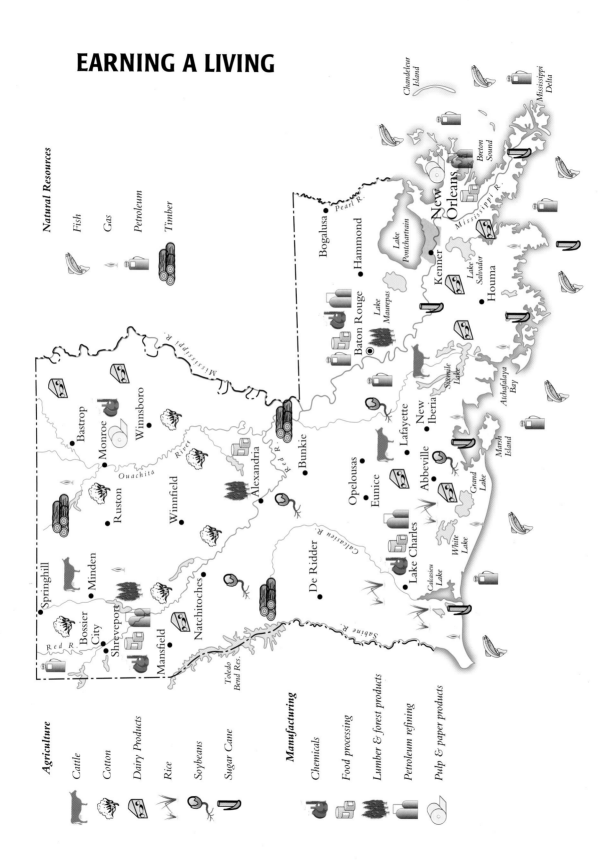

**Natural Resources**

Fish
Gas
Petroleum
Timber

**Agriculture**

Cattle
Cotton
Dairy Products
Rice
Soybeans
Sugar Cane

**Manufacturing**

Chemicals
Food processing
Lumber & forest products
Petroleum refining
Pulp & paper products

Chandeleur Island
Mississippi Delta
Breton Sound
New Orleans
Kenner
Houma
Lake Salvador
Lake Pontchartrain
Bogalusa
Hammond
Baton Rouge
Lake Maurepas
Lafayette
New Iberia
Spanish Lake
Atchafalaya Bay
Marsh Island
Grand Lake
Opelousas
Eunice
Abbeville
Lake Charles
White Lake
Calcasieu Lake
De Ridder
Pearl R.
Mississippi R.
Bastrop
Monroe
Winnsboro
Ruston
Winnfield
Alexandria
Bunkie
Ouachita River
Red R.
Calcasieu R.
Sabine R.
Toledo Bend Res.
Springhill
Minden
Bossier City
Shreveport
Natchitoches
Mansfield
Red R.

# 1992 GROSS STATE PRODUCT: $80 MILLION

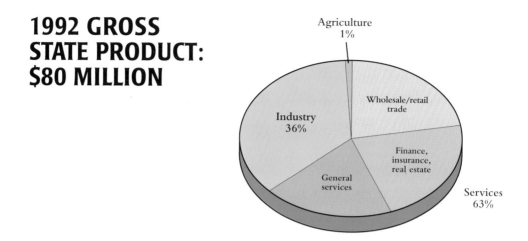

Agriculture 1%

Wholesale/retail trade

Industry 36%

Finance, insurance, real estate

General services

Services 63%

Fortunately, there are signs that things are changing for the better. The largest sector of the state's economy—and the nation's, too—consists of the service industries. People who work for banks, private hospitals, advertising agencies, and stores all have jobs in the service industry. So do waiters and other people who work in the tourist industry, which is an important part of the Louisiana economy. In 1996, service industries accounted for about two-thirds of Louisiana's gross state product and that percentage is likely to grow in the years to come.

"New Orleans is one of the friendliest cities in the south," brags a long-time New Orleans resident. "We just love having people come here to enjoy our food and music. Which is a good thing, because we really need the money they bring in." Louisiana's reputation as the jazz capital of the world, its fine restaurants, and its unique geographical features combine to attract tourists by the millions: Louisiana's tourist industry currently employs more than 87,000 workers and brings in an estimated $5.2 billion every year.

Economists think that oil and gas prices will rise in the next ten years or so. Since mining is the single most important economic activity in the state, this trend also means more money for Louisiana. The state contains just under 10 percent of all known U.S. oil reserves and is the country's third largest producer of petroleum. It has even more natural gas, producing just over one-quarter of all U.S. supplies. Louisiana also is one of the few states that does not severely restrict offshore drilling for oil and gas. While that may be bad for the environment, it is good for the economy.

Louisiana's lumber and paper industries will probably expand in the years to come, and for the same reason. The state has more than 13.9 million acres of pine, oak, gum, and cypress trees. Most Louisiana timber grows on private, rather than federal property and thus is subject to fewer restrictions. Hence, timber can be harvested much more easily. In fact, in 1995, five lumber and paper plants announced they were relocating or expanding there.

Another booming industry is commercial fishing. More than 25 percent of all the fish caught in America is caught in Louisiana waters. The state is the largest producer of shrimp and oysters and also has lots of crab, red snapper, and tuna. The Atchafalaya River Basin swamp produces millions of crawfish—small lobsterlike crustaceans—every year.

Louisianians also hope to benefit from an expansion of international trade in the coming decades. The state's position on the Gulf of Mexico and its proximity to Latin America mean that its petrochemicals and manufactured goods can be shipped efficiently to important markets. Louisiana's five major ports already handle roughly four hundred million tons of cargo each year, and more

*Some 100 million pounds of crawfish—miniature lobsterlike crustaceans—are harvested from Louisiana waters every year.*

than 25 percent of the nation's waterborne exports pass through the state.

Finally, Louisiana is home to a number of high-tech industries. Three major aerospace corporations have divisions in Louisiana: Martin Marietta employs more than 2,500 people in New Orleans to construct the external fuel tanks for NASA's space shuttle

# CELEBRATING NATURE'S BOUNTY

From Louisiana's rich farmland and waters come many delicious foodstuffs, and Louisianians take every opportunity to celebrate this bounty during fairs and festivals across the state.

Louisiana produces 99 percent of all the crawfish in the country, a fact that the town of Breaux Bridge—the "Crawfish Capital of the World"—applauds with gusto every May during **Crawfish Festival.** Crowley, the center of Louisiana's rice-growing district, throws an **International Rice Festival,** complete with a crowned Rice Queen who flings bags of rice from a colorful float during the annual parade.

In March, the town of Amite throws a festival for the oyster, that delectable crustacean Southerners love to fry and put in sandwiches called po'boys or eat raw on a half-shell with hot sauce. Gonzales, a town located in the heart of Cajun country and the self-proclaimed "Jambalaya Capital of the World," serves thousands of people healthy helpings of the spicy sausage-and-rice stew during the **Jambalaya Festival.**

Strawberries, blueberries, peaches, corn, catfish, crabs, gumbo . . . Louisianians honor them all with parades, cook-offs, and other festivities that bring communities together and attract visitors from all over the state.

program. The Boeing Corporation in Lake Charles employs about two thousand people to repair jet aircraft, and a division of Rockwell International operates an aircraft center in Shreveport.

## . . . AND LOUISIANA LIVING

Louisiana has one of the lowest state income tax rates in the country and does not ask its citizens to pay property taxes. Its sales tax on goods people buy in stores is only 4 percent. Some people like paying so little in taxes. Others think that the government needs to bring in more money to pay for much needed public services.

Indeed, Louisiana faces a number of tough problems. The health and welfare of its citizens—particularly its children—is probably the most pressing concern. Among all states, Louisiana has the most children living in poverty (32 percent) and the highest rate

*More than 25 percent of the nation's waterborne exports pass through Louisiana, including more than 40 percent of all the grain exported from the United States.*

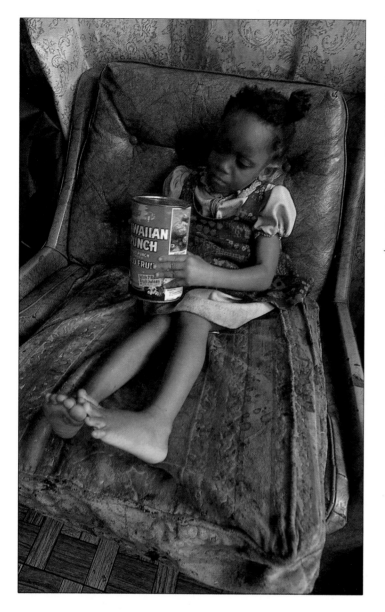

*Poverty remains a sad fact of life for more children living in Louisiana than anywhere else in the country. One in five Louisiana children lacks health insurance, and about the same number live in single-parent families.*

of infant mortality. Louisiana ranks fiftieth—or lowest—among all states in the general health of its population. Nevertheless, spending for health care and human services (which includes welfare payments to the unemployed) accounts for more than 40 percent of the state's total expenditures.

In 1994, the Big Easy became known as the Murder Capital of the World. Its murder rate was a shocking 114 percent higher than the national average. "Sometimes I'm scared to walk alone at night," admits Susan Peters, a nurse from New Orleans. "I carry a whistle and take my dog with me whenever possible. But I love living here, and my friends and I go out a lot together. You just have to know what neighborhoods are safe and which ones to avoid."

# TEN LARGEST CITIES

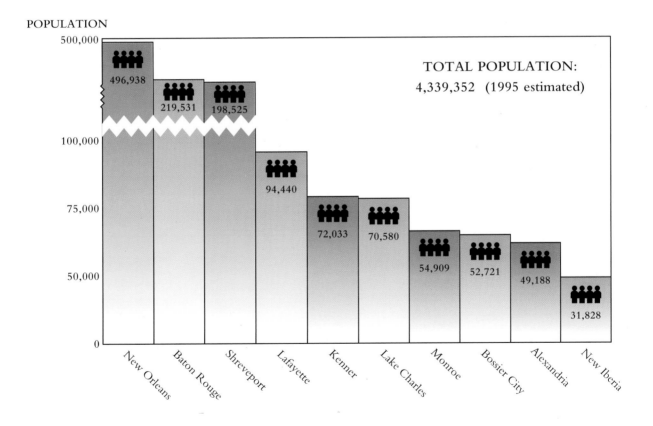

*An influx of illegal drugs combined with an increase in poverty and unemployment have made New Orleans the "Murder Capital of the World," a fact that citizens and law enforcement personnel alike are now fighting to reverse.*

Most crimes were committed in New Orleans and other big cities, and many of them were related to illegal drugs. Fortunately, crime rates decreased in 1995. Much of this was due to increased spending for public safety and corrections services. The government spent about $520 million on its law enforcement efforts in 1996.

Education is another prime concern for the people of Louisiana. Today, more than 770,000 children attend prekindergarten to Grade 12 in Louisiana schools. The government spends about $4,290 every year to educate each pupil. That's about 8 percent below the national average of $5,720. Recently, the government established a "Goals 2000" committee to help oversee improvements in educational standards throughout the state.

As for higher education, many of Louisiana's colleges and universities have earned outstanding reputations. Tulane University in New Orleans and Louisiana State University in Baton Rouge are two excellent liberal arts schools that attract students from all over the world.

"I'm here from London and I find it fascinating," says an economics student at Tulane. "It's hard to study sometimes because of all the night life and music the city has to offer, but I feel like I'm getting a first-class education, too."

Grambling College and Dillard and Southern Universities were all originally founded as schools for blacks. Today, all of Louisiana's institutions of higher education are integrated.

With its valuable store of natural resources and a population of hard-working citizens, Louisiana looks to the future with energy and optimism—two qualities never in short supply.

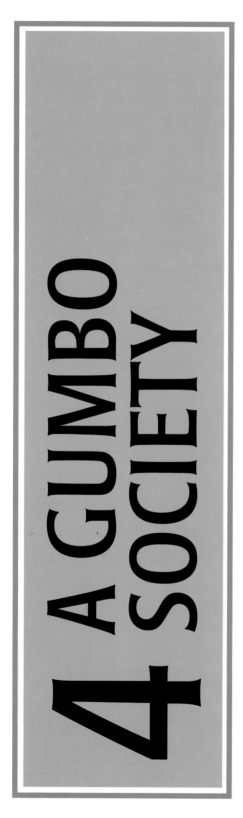

# 4 A GUMBO SOCIETY

*The Crawfish Festival in Breaux Bridge*

"My childhood in New Orleans was like growing up in America and not being in America," writer Anne Rice once told a reporter. Visitors who come to Louisiana from other parts of the United States often feel the same way: The cultures they encounter here are usually very different from anything they've experienced at home.

As soon as you step off the plane, you feel as though you've entered a foreign land. Loudspeakers impart information in both French and English. Advertisements for "boudin," "étouffée," and other odd-sounding foods line the corridors. Music called zydeco plays on the radio with a foot-stomping "ka-chank, ka-chank" sound you've never heard before. When you look at a map, the place names look just as strange: the Ouachita River, Tchoupitoulas Street, Natchitoches. Porters and cab drivers greet you with "Where y'at?" spoken in a peculiar Southern drawl. Within a few short minutes, you've had a glimpse of Louisiana's remarkable diversity.

Locals like to call the state a "simmering pot of spicy gumbo." A hearty stew of vegetables, seafood, meats, and spices, gumbo does indeed make an apt metaphor for Louisiana society today. Native Americans, Europeans, Africans and Caribbean islanders, Cajuns, and a myriad of other groups have each added their own special ingredients to the pot.

## NATIVE CULTURE: AN ENDURING LEGACY

Although the arrival of the Europeans nearly put an end to their flourishing civilization, the natives of Louisiana were crucial to the state's development. It was they who taught the French and Spanish how to fish from the region's lakes, harvest the delta soil, and navigate its great rivers. Native languages also became an important part of Louisiana's heritage. Thousands of streets, parks, towns, and parishes throughout the state have Indian names.

Louisiana celebrates its Native American history in several museums. The Cabildo in New Orleans explores the day-to-day life of both Indians and settlers. In Avoyelles Parish, you'll find the Tunica-Biloxi Regional Indian Center and Museum, which contains a collection of native artifacts from Louisiana's colonial period.

Today, approximately twelve thousand natives call Louisiana

## ETHNIC LOUISIANA

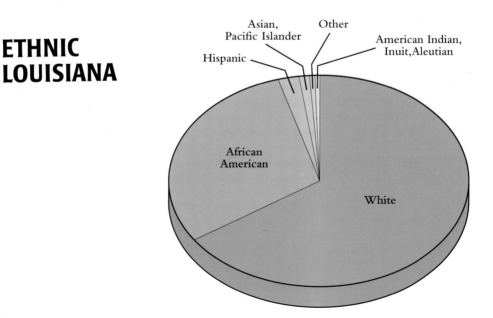

# GUMBO: A POT OF PLENTY

There are as many different recipes for gumbo as there are Louisiana chefs. This one comes from Mary Ann Weilbaecher, who owns the elegant Josephine Guest House in New Orleans' Garden District.

## The Gumbo Base

1-1/4 lb. Creole smoked sausage (or any hot, smoked sausage), sliced 1/2 inch thick

1/2 lb. lean ham, cut into 1/2-inch cubes

1 four-pound chicken, cut up

1/2 cup chopped green pepper

1/2 cup thinly sliced scallion tops

2 tbs. minced parsley

1 tbs. minced garlic

2 cups chopped onion

## The Roux

2/3 cup vegetable oil

1/2 cup flour

## The Liquid and the Seasonings

2 qt. cold water

3 tsp. salt

1 tsp. black pepper

1/8 tsp. cayenne

1-1/4 tsp. dried thyme

3 whole bay leaves, crushed

2-1/2 to 3 tbs. file powder (Found in some supermarkets. Leave it out if you can't find it.)

Assemble the ingredients for the gumbo base, then heat the oil in a heavy 8-quart pot over high heat. (Ask an adult for help when using the stove.) Brown the chicken parts, turning them several times. Remove to a heated platter and place in a 175° oven to keep warm.

Make the roux (paste) by gradually adding the flour to the oil, stirring constantly. Reduce the heat and cook, always stirring, until a medium brown roux is formed. When the roux reaches the right color, immediately add 1/4 cup of water, all ingredients (including the chicken) except the file powder and mix thoroughly. Stir in the rest of the water, then raise the heat and bring to a boil. Lower the heat and simmer the gumbo for 50 minutes or until the chicken is tender. Stir frequently. Remove the pot from the heat, then add the file powder. Let the gumbo stand five minutes, then serve over boiled rice.

home—just about the same number that lived here four centuries ago. The Houma of Terrebone Parish make up the largest group of natives. The Chitimacha and the Coushatta live in the north. In Louisiana, and throughout the United States, native people remain among the poorest and most isolated of all ethnic groups. In recent years, both the Chitimacha and the Coushatta tribes have opened gaming casinos on tribal land in hopes of boosting their economy.

## CREOLE ELEGANCE AND SPICE

It is hard to imagine what the French and Spanish settlers (known as Creoles) thought when they first confronted the junglelike landscape and humidity of Louisiana. One early settler, Colonel James Creecy, wrote of his first exposure to the land, "The wildness and desolation will ever remain deeply engraved in my memory . . . a dreary home for alligators, mud turtles, catfish, and sea birds." Indeed, a more different environment from that of the sophisticated cities of Paris or Madrid could not exist.

Nevertheless, the Creoles quickly adapted to their new home. They built Catholic churches and cathedrals, established schools for their children, and set up a legal and political system. Many of these institutions survive today: Almost every town in southern Louisiana is graced by a church in its center, counties are still called parishes, and the legal system retains its French legacy of the Napoleonic Code.

Even more important, the French and Spanish made several lasting contributions to Louisiana's cultural heritage. Creoles

The heritage of the Coushatta Indians is kept alive through festivals and tribal re-enactments.

Many former plantations, such as this one in Shreveport, are now living museums. "Visiting one of the Creole plantations is like taking a step back in time," remarks Elizabeth Gold, a tourist from New England. "Here in Louisiana you can really see what life was like two centuries ago."

founded the state's first symphonies, opera companies, and ballet troupes. Their architects designed homes and laid out towns based on French and Spanish models which still define Louisiana's landscape today.

Perhaps the most enduring Creole legacy is a social one. The traditional Creole love of food, drink, and conversation remains very much a part of the modern Louisiana lifestyle. "We all love to talk and to tell stories," admits New Orleans native Stephanie Fournier. "My ancestors came here sometime in the 1700s. The stories they passed down from one generation to the next—about everything: food, politics, you name it—could fill a lot of books."

## THE LOUISIANA BLACK EXPERIENCE

Since colonial times, African Americans have contributed much to Louisiana's culture and society. Most of the earliest blacks in Louisiana came as slaves. Louisiana became dependent upon the slave labor that harvested its cotton, sugar, and rice crops. Life for slaves in this humid, mosquito-ridden land was brutal, because of the harshness of its climate and its slaveowners. "Louisiana was considered by the slaves as a place of slaughter," wrote Jacob Stoyer, a slave who lived in North Carolina, "so those who were going [there] did not expect to see their friends again."

At the same time, Louisiana had the largest population of free blacks in the South before the Civil War. Some arrived later, as free men and women, from other parts of North America, Europe, the Caribbean islands, and Africa. And some slaves were granted their freedom by their white owners. In 1856, the state supreme court ruled that "in the eyes of the Louisiana law there is . . . all the difference between a free man of color and a slave that there is between a white man and a slave."

In fact, several free African Americans became wealthy and powerful enough to own their own plantations. Cyprian Ricard was the richest free person of color before the Civil War. He owned two cotton plantations in Iberville Parish. Marie Thérèse, also known by her African name of Coincoin, had an even more fascinating story. A child of African parents, Marie Thérèse was freed at the age of thirty-eight after being a white man's mistress for many years. She inherited a small plot of land that she built into a great plantation—so great, in fact, that she earned enough money to buy the freedom of her still-enslaved children. Her plantation, called Melrose, developed into a large community of free blacks near Natchitoches in central Louisiana.

African Americans shared their cultures with the other citizens of the state. Their languages mixed with French, Spanish, and Native American dialects. Blacks certainly added spice to the gumbo pot— and quite literally at that. They contributed the use of okra (a sticky podlike vegetable) and the spice sassafras (also called file) to Louisiana cooking.

Without question, jazz remains the most enduring contribution made by blacks in Louisiana. Jazz developed out of a mingling of musical traditions blacks brought with them from Africa and the Caribbean and blended with European music they heard in Louisiana. Louis Armstrong, Jelly Roll Morton, and Sidney Bechet are just a few of the jazz innovators who were born and bred in Louisiana. Rhythm and blues, a related musical form that uses

# MARIE LAVEAU, VOODOO QUEEN

"Believe it or not, strange as it seems, she made a fortune selling voodoo . . . Marie Laveau, she was a voodoo queen way down yonder in New Orleans."

The song called "Marie Laveau" tells the story of one of New Orleans' most infamous and mysterious figures. Marie Laveau was born about 1794 and lived as a *gens de couleur libre*, or free person of color, during the nineteenth century. She was best known, though, for practicing voodoo, a religion with roots in Africa, Haiti, Cuba, Trinidad, and Brazil. Voodoo combines a belief in one god with a belief in various kinds of spirits. Laveau acted as a mambo, or priestess. On behalf of her clients, she would invoke the spirits by drumming, dancing, and feasting, then allow a spirit to possess her. While in a trance, Laveau would then pass along advice or perform cures created by the spirit. For this, wealthy members of Louisiana society paid her very well.

Marie Laveau died in 1851. She was buried at midnight by the light of the moon in St. Louis Cemetery No. 1 in New Orleans. Her grave remains a highly popular tourist attraction, as does the Voodoo Museum in New Orleans.

*"Music is everywhere in New Orleans. There's hardly a corner in the French Quarter that doesn't offer a blare of a trumpet or a wail of a saxophone, " boasts one of the city's many street musicians. "And jazz is still king."*

more voices and different tempos than jazz, also had roots in the Louisiana black experience. Fats Domino and Professor Longhair helped develop this foot-stomping predecessor of rock and roll.

Today, blacks make up more than 30 percent of Louisiana's population. They live and work in every part of the state, but most call south Louisiana home. Richard Sadlier, the parish priest of the largely African-American church St. Benedict the Black, in Donaldsonville, remarks about the strong feelings for home shared by many of his neighbors. "Yes, [people] might go off to Texas or Los Angeles, but they always come back. People born here come back and die here. It's in their roots."

The Louisiana black experience is celebrated throughout the state: The New Orleans Museum of Art features a large African collection containing tribal masks and stories of ancient native

*Clementine Hunter's* Washing Clothes *is an excellent example of Louisiana's folk art tradition.*

customs. At Melrose Plantation in Natchitoches, you can not only learn more about Coincoin, but also see the paintings of Clementine Hunter, one of Louisiana's most renowned painters of folk art.

## THE CAJUN EXPERIENCE

In 1755, a large group of families from Halifax, Nova Scotia, arrived in southern Louisiana. They joined a small community of other French Canadians already living on farms along the Mississippi River, Bayou Teche, and Bayou Lafourche. These people came to Louisiana because they had nowhere else to go. They and their ancestors had lived in Acadia—the French colonies in what is today Canada—until the British took over the region during the Seven Years War. The British then exiled any French Canadian who did not renounce the Roman Catholic religion and swear allegiance to the Crown.

Once in Louisiana, the Acadians developed a unique culture. Called Cajuns (a corruption of the original French pronunciation of Acadian), they established self-contained villages along the bayous. They lived off the land, hunting, fishing, and farming. Cajun French, still spoken today, uses words and grammar derived from a mixture of traditional French, English, Spanish, African, and Native American languages. The Cajun dialect is completely oral— no written dictionaries or grammar books exist—and yet it remains alive and vibrant in Louisiana today.

Cajuns have also added some interesting culinary delights to the Louisiana pot. Perhaps more than any other group in the state, Cajuns have used Louisiana's wildlife in their cooking. Alligator,

*A historic Acadian, or Cajun, village near Lafayette*

crawfish, and turtles might never have made their way onto the
Louisiana table had it not been for the Cajun flair in cooking them.

Music, too, is a part of the Cajun heritage. Using medieval
French music as their base, Cajuns wrote new songs of loneliness
and ill-fated love, a reaction to their brutal exile. At first, they
carried no instruments, but soon the fiddle (or violin) became their
central instrument. They also used the frottoir—a washboardlike

instrument—that made a "ka-chonk, ka-chonk" sound for rhythm. Later, they added the accordion to the mix.

Cajun music has a cousin—zydeco—which was influenced by folk and rhythm and blues. Stanley Dural, the leader of the band Buckwheat Zydeco, described the music this way: "You add a little blues, a little soul, a little rock 'n' roll, and a little jazz and mix it all in. Sometimes you can hear five different types of music in one song."

Although some Cajuns still make their living off the land, most have moved to the cities along with the rest of Louisiana society. Their culture, however, remains very much alive throughout southern Louisiana. Louisiana folklorist Barry Jean Ancelet speaks to the "uncanny adaptability" of the Cajuns. "Cajuns have always been able to chew up change, swallow the palatable parts, and spit out the rest."

Today, Louisiana's population is among the most diverse in the nation. People from all over the world—from Albania to Zimbabwe—have joined the state's founding groups to give Louisiana one of the most richly textured cultures in our nation.

O bébé/on va danser/Danser, danser le jig français/ Comme les temps, les temps passer. *"Oh baby, let's dance, let's dance the French jig. How the time, the time passes."* So go the lyrics to a Cajun melody, its beat marked by the ka-chank, ka-chank of the washboard, or frottoir.

# 5 LOUISIANA HALL OF FAME

It might be something in the fragrant air or maybe something in the spicy food. It could be the "let the good times roll" atmosphere or the warmth of its citizens. No matter the cause—and it's probably a combination of all these things and more—from Louisiana come some of the brightest and most talented athletes, chefs, and writers in the world. Let's meet a few of them now.

## PLAYING THE LOUISIANA WAY

Visitors and residents alike call Louisiana the Sportsman's Paradise because of its many opportunities for fishing, hunting, boating, and hiking. But Louisiana is proud of its professional athletes, too, who have risen to the very tops of their fields.

**Ron Guidry** played baseball for the New York Yankees during the 1970s. His fast pitching earned him the nickname "Louisiana Lightnin'" as well as the 1978 Cy Young Award for best pitcher in the American League. Despite all his years in New York and traveling on the road, he never lost his love for Louisiana. He even had his family and friends mail him food from back home, especially the special blend of coffee beans and chicory for which New Orleans is famous. "I can't go too long without good coffee," he told a reporter. When he retired from baseball, he returned to the town of Lafayette to raise his family.

*Known to his fans as "Louisiana Lightnin'," to reporters as the "Ragin' Cajun," and to his teammates as "Gator," Ron Guidry pitched against some of the hardest hitters in baseball and came out a winner. He once said, "You don't have to be big to win. . . . Size doesn't make any difference if you don't scare, if you're brave."*

**Bill Russell**, star center with the Boston Celtics, led his basketball team to eleven championships from 1956 to 1969. Russell was born in 1934 in the northern Louisiana city of Monroe, at a time when prejudice toward African Americans was particularly strong. Russell told reporters that his experiences with discrimination as a black child in the South helped to make him more assertive about demanding his civil rights as an adult. Russell was elected to the Basketball Hall of Fame in 1974, then went on to coach basketball and work as a sports announcer in the years that followed.

*Considered one of the finest defensive players of all time, basketball star Bill Russell grew up in Monroe, Louisiana.*

## LOUISIANA KITCHENS

Good cooking and hearty eating are as much a part of the Louisiana experience as heated political discussions and lazy days spent along the bayou. It should come as no surprise, then, that some of the nation's most talented chefs hail from the Pelican State.

**Paul Prudhomme** is perhaps Louisiana's most famous chef. Born and raised on a farm in Opelousas, Louisiana, Prudhomme opened his first restaurant in New Orleans in 1979. Called K-Paul's, it was the first major New Orleans restaurant to feature spicy Cajun food like blackened fish, gumbo, and jambalaya.

K-Paul's soon became one of the best and most popular Cajun restaurants in New Orleans. "Food is my passion, and my mission in life is to make your dinner better," he once said, and he certainly has dedicated himself to that goal. Videos, cookbooks, and a line of specialty spices have brought Cajun cooking—and the Prudhomme name—into kitchens across the country and around the world.

*Paul Prudhomme's portly frame and friendly grin greet millions of diners when they enter his New Orleans restaurant, K-Paul's, or buy one of his cookbooks chock full of delicious Cajun recipes.*

# LOUISIANA COOKING DICTIONARY

A Louisiana menu is frequently filled with words the average American has never seen. This guide may help you decide what to eat—and how to pronounce it—when you visit the Pelican State. Please note: Pronunciations are highly variable, from community to community—even family to family. And for those of you who know a little French, keep in mind that the accent in Louisiana is *not* classical French, but rather influenced by the unique mix of cultures and languages found in the state.

**Andouille and Boudin** (ahn-DOU-ee and boo-DAN): two types of Cajun sausage. Andouille is made with pork, and boudin with pork and rice. Both types may be quite spicy.

**Beignet** (BEN-yay): a fritter (ball of fried dough) covered with sugar and eaten as a breakfast doughnut.

**Etouffée** (eh-too-FAY): a method of preparing shrimp, crawfish, and other fish with tomatoes and spices. Etouffée is served over rice.

**File** (FEE-lay): ground sassafras used to spice many Cajun sauces.

**Gumbo** (GUM-bo): a spicy stew made with okra, pork, chicken, seafood, and/or wild game. The word "gumbo" is thought to come from the African word "guin-gombo" which means okra, or the Choctaw word "kombo" which is the word for sassafras, an ingredient in most gumbos.

**Jambalaya** (JUM-ba-lie-ya): a dish made with rice, chopped vegetables, pork, sausage (usually Andouille sausage) and seafood. Jambalaya can be spicy or mild, depending on the type of sausage used.

**Muffaletta** (muff-a-LAH-duh): Italian sandwich stuffed with different kinds of meats and cheeses, frequently dressed with garlic dressing, herbed olives, and tomatoes.

**Po'boy** (PO-boy): a hero sandwich stuffed with fried oysters, meats, or other fillings.

**Roux** (roo): the base of most Creole sauces made of flour browned in butter. In fact, almost every Creole recipe begins with the words "First you make a roux." The trick to making a good roux, most cooks will tell you, is stirring: You have to cook the flour slowly to a nutty brown without letting it get so hot it turns black.

Bringing more of a Creole (old European) flavor to New Orleans dining, the **Brennan Family** has been active in the city's restaurant scene since 1946, when a restaurant called Brennan's opened in the French Quarter, the oldest part of the city. Four Brennan children—Dick, Ella, John, and Dottie—opened another establishment, Commander's Palace, uptown in the city's elegant Garden District. Both Brennan's and Commander's Palace feature classic Creole cooking and are known for their fine service and hospitality.

"In spite of all the changes going on around us," Ella Brennan recently told a group of restauranteurs, "this business is still basically about people." This attitude has allowed the Brennan restaurants to maintain a warm and inviting atmosphere while serving remarkable food prepared by world-class chefs.

## THE WRITERS

Writers have long been inspired by the sights, sounds, and sensibilities of Louisiana. Indeed, some of America's greatest writers were either born in Louisiana or adopted the state as home during a crucial period in their creative lives.

**William Faulkner** lived most of his life in Mississippi, but wrote his first novel, *Soldier's Pay*, while staying in New Orleans' French Quarter. He stayed with Sherwood Anderson, who lived in an apartment in the Pontalba Building, a historic apartment house with iron-lace balconies. Faulkner later wrote that the building looked as though it had been "cut from black paper and pasted flat on a green sky."

**Truman Capote** was born in New Orleans in 1924 and returned

*"Don't be fooled. He looks like a ten-year-old angel," said Jean Cocteau of fellow author and New Orleans native Truman Capote, "but he is ageless and has a very wicked mind."*

to the city often throughout his life. In fact, Capote considered himself to be very much a Southerner even though he spent much of his adult life in New York City and Los Angeles. His first novel, *Other Voices, Other Rooms,* tells the story of a young boy's coming of age in a small Southern town. Capote wrote this book at the tender age of seventeen, yet many critics consider it to be his masterpiece. *A Tree of Night and Other Stories, The Grass Harp,* and *Breakfast at Tiffany's* are also highly acclaimed works of fiction. In 1966, Capote became famous as the author of *In Cold Blood,* a non-fiction look at the murder of a Kansas family. All of Capote's writings are richly evocative of both spirit and place. "It's awful for me to endure reality," he once said. "I just can't stand it. It's boredom." The imaginative worlds he created continue to enchant his readers.

Lillian Hellman, one of the greatest playwrights of the twentieth century, was born in New Orleans in 1905. Like Truman Capote, she spent much of her life in New York City and Los Angeles, but considered New Orleans to be her home town. In 1934, Hellman's first drama opened on Broadway. Called *The Children's Hour*, it became a hit. Many of Hellman's plays dealt with political issues, including *Watch on the Rhine*, published in 1941, which dramatized the fight of a brave German opposed to the rule of Adolph Hitler. *Watch on the Rhine* won the New York Drama Critics Circle Award, as did her 1960 play *Toys in the Attic*.

More recently, Louisiana has produced a number of mystery and horror writers who bring alive Louisiana's seedier and eerier side. Two of the most prolific are **Anne Rice** and **James Lee Burke**. Rice brings the vampire Lestat alive in her series of novels called the Vampire Chronicles. Her descriptions of New Orleans' cemeteries surrounded by live oaks dripping with Spanish moss create a creepy atmosphere for the spooky goings-on. **James Lee Burke**, born and raised on the Louisiana Gulf Coast, created the character Dave Robicheaux, a Cajun detective for the New Orleans Police Department who later becomes a private eye exploring the Big Easy's underworld of crime and vice.

## THE BEAT OF THE BAYOU

Music is an integral part of Louisiana culture. Many people consider New Orleans to be the birthplace of jazz. Blues, folk, and rock and roll have all been influenced by musicians born or trained in Louisiana.

**Louis Armstrong** was born in a poor section of New Orleans in 1900 and grew up to become the most popular jazz performer of all time. His musical career began at the age of five, when he sang in the streets of New Orleans for pennies. Later, after being sent to a reform school for shooting off a gun on New Year's Eve, he learned to play the bugle, cornet, and trumpet, as well as to write his own lyrics and music. In 1922, Armstrong moved to Chicago to make his first jazz recording. During a recording session, he dropped his sheet music and instead of stopping, he improvised by singing a

*Louis "Satchmo" Armstrong, who spent most of his childhood in a New Orleans orphanage, grew up to become "America's Ambassador of Jazz."*

## BOOGY DOWN ON THE BAYOU

Every year during the last week in April and the first week in May, millions of music lovers from all over the world come to Louisiana for the New Orleans Jazz and Heritage Festival. "I come here every year, and every year it gets better," claims Michael Infante, a guitar player and music lover from New England. "The people, the music, the food, the city . . . it's amazing. No one should miss coming here at least once in their lives."

More than four thousand musicians, cooks, and craftspeople welcome more than four hundred thousand people every year. The ten-day festival includes daily concerts performed by the best jazz, gospel, rhythm and blues, and zydeco musicians in the world. Most concerts take place at the Fair Grounds Race Track. Music resounds from eleven stages while marching brass bands wind their way through the crowds. Cajun crafts are on display, and the food that has made Louisiana famous—jambalaya, crawfish served a million different ways, po'boy sandwiches stuffed with oysters—is available in booths that dot the field. At night, performers entertain in clubs around the city. In the words of the *Boston Globe* newspaper, the Jazz Fest has become "America's Best Festival," both a spirited celebration of music and a showcase for Louisiana's unique heritage.

series of wordless syllables. Called "scat," this style of singing became a central part of the jazz tradition. His soulful renditions of such classics as "What a Wonderful World" and "I've Got a Heart Full of Rhythm" and duets with another great scat singer, Ella Fitzgerald, brought him great popularity and acclaim. "If it weren't for him, there wouldn't be any of us," jazz trumpeter Dizzy Gillespie said of Louisiana's favorite son.

The list of jazz and blues innovators from the New Orleans area is long. **Huddie Ledbetter**, also known as Leadbelly, was born in 1888 in Mooringsport, Louisiana. His early life was rough, and he spent many years in prison for murder, attempted murder, and assault. The songs he wrote and the music he played stemming from his pain and struggle influenced not only jazz, but folk and popular music as well. New Orleans native **Sidney Bechet** taught himself to play the clarinet at the age of six and became one of the leading jazz saxophonists and clarinetists in the country during the 1940s and 1950s.

**Mahalia Jackson** brought gospel music to the rest of America and the world with her energetic and emotional style. Born in New Orleans, she first sang in local Baptist churches, then moved to Chicago where her popularity surged. In 1950, she made her debut at Carnegie Hall in New York City. During the civil rights movement of the 1950s and 1960s, Mahalia Jackson lent her support by singing at the rallies of Reverend Martin Luther King Jr. and at his funeral.

Today, New Orleans continues to produce some of the world's most talented and popular musicians. In recent decades, the **Marsalis Family** is living proof that New Orleans still has a gift for producing some of the world's most talented musicians. Father Ellis Marsalis, a jazz pianist, and his two sons, Wynton and Branford, who play the trumpet and the saxophone, have a world-wide following of dedicated listeners. *New Orleans* magazine wrote that "If New Orleans' best gift to nineteenth-century music was jazz, then New Orleans' best gift to twentieth-century music might be the entire Marsalis family."

*Wynton Marsalis, seen here blowing his trumpet at the 1984 Grammy awards, once described jazz as the "ultimate expression of democracy . . . because when it's played properly it shows you how the individual can negotiate the greatest amount of personal freedom and put it humbly at the service of a group conception."*

Among the many other Louisiana musicians performing today are **The Neville Brothers**, who combine blues and zydeco to create their own unique sound; **Dr. John**, the pianist and composer of New Orleans-style jazz and blues; and **Harry Connick Jr.**, a singer and piano player with suave good looks and a style that reminds many of the young Frank Sinatra.

The creativity and vigor of the people of Louisiana are no doubt influenced by the state's magnificent natural resources—its bayous and Gulf shore beaches, its lively cities and quaint villages. In the next chapter, you'll catch a glimpse of what makes Louisiana so special.

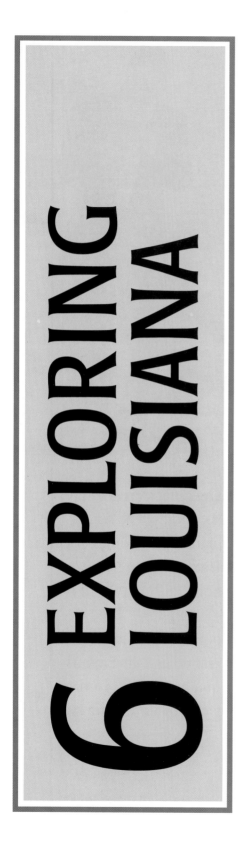

# 6 EXPLORING LOUISIANA

Many people assume that Louisiana has only two landscapes: a hilly, pine tree-covered north and a swampy, humid south. In truth, the north has its share of swampland and alligators; the south has lush farmland and rolling hills; and nearly every city, town, and bayou village along the way has something special to offer.

People come from all over the world to visit Louisiana. Most of them arrive by plane at New Orleans International Airport. Let's start our tour of the Pelican State right there.

## THE BIG EASY

The twenty-five-minute ride from the airport to downtown New Orleans will give you a good idea of what life in Louisiana is like today. Just sixty years ago, Louisiana had only three thousand miles of paved roads. Fifty-five thousand miles of roads and highways now crisscross the state. You'll ride on one of those highways—Highway 10—south toward the city.

On the way, you'll see a typical urban sprawl—small businesses, stores, and factories line the highway, and cars speed by on the route that also leads to and from Baton Rouge, the state capital. Soon, the gleaming skyscrapers of downtown New Orleans come into view.

"I love coming home to Louisiana and driving into New Orleans," says Joe Peters, a physician who lives in a suburb of the state's largest city. "Right beside the highway, in front of the factories and stores, is the Atchafalaya swamp, looking as muddy and mysterious as anything." Throughout the state, you'll notice that modern industry sits alongside both rugged nature and historic elegance.

Cypress trees and the dark green waters that hide what lurks beneath let you know you've arrived in the Big Easy. As you approach the city, you have one more treat—a ride over the longest bridge in the world. The Lake Pontchartrain Causeway, built in 1956, spans twenty-four miles of this six-hundred-square-mile body of water.

**The French Quarter.** Once you've arrived in New Orleans, your adventure really begins. You're at once enveloped by new sights, sounds, and aromas. Novelist Anne Rice describes what makes her hometown so special this way: "It's the color of the sky—the color of the banana trees—the flowers—the heart. It's walking, breathing, being here."

Let's go first to the city's oldest section, which is filled with fine examples of eighteenth- and nineteenth-century Creole architecture. Called the French Quarter or the Vieux Carré (Old Square), its narrow streets are lined with picturesque homes, hotels, shops, and restaurants. Residents adorn the railings of their cast-iron balconies with flowers and gather around fountains bubbling in hidden courtyards.

Bourbon Street is the most famous avenue in the Quarter, and it's usually jammed with people enjoying its sights and sounds.

*"In this part of New Orleans, you are practically always just around the corner, or a few doors down the street, from a tinny piano being played with the infatuated fluency of brown fingers." So wrote Tennessee Williams about the French Quarter in his play* A Streetcar Named Desire.

*The legacy of the Spanish period can be seen in the elegant cast-iron railings that adorn balconies throughout the French Quarter of New Orleans.*

Jazz and rhythm-and-blues musicians perform both inside the Quarter's many clubs and outside on its sidewalks. Preservation Hall, where Dixieland jazz great Pete Fountain often plays, is perhaps the most famous city jazz club.

The center of the French Quarter is Jackson Square. The focal point of the original city, Jackson Square contains several historic buildings. St. Louis Cathedral, the oldest cathedral in the United States, dominates the square with its majestic spires. The Cabildo, now housing a branch of the Louisiana State Museum, was the seat of the Spanish government in the early nineteenth century. In the square itself, fortune tellers deal tarot cards, artists paint portraits, and musicians play the blues. One of the best ways to enjoy New Orleans is to stroll through this open-air arena. "This is the first place I come when I visit this city," a tourist from Illinois remarks. "It takes the Midwest right out of me!"

On the other side of Jackson Square lies the Mississippi River. Huge oil tankers and other commercial vessels ply these waters, as do riverboat casinos, tourist steamboats, and pleasure craft. The sight of the "Big Muddy"—so named because of its brown color and the tons of sediment it carries—is awesome.

With all of its attractions, many visitors never leave the French Quarter. But New Orleans has much more to offer. The busy commercial Canal Street marks the division between the French Quarter and "uptown." The first Anglo-Saxon plantation owners developed this part of the city in the early nineteenth century.

**Uptown on the Trolley.** To go uptown, you can take a charming streetcar that travels from Canal Street all the way

# MARDI GRAS: LET THE GOOD TIMES ROLL

For about ten days, starting in January or February, the city of New Orleans hosts the largest Mardi Gras festival in the world. Marked by a series of elaborate parades, wild parties, elegant balls, and merrymaking of all kinds, Mardi Gras in New Orleans has been described as "The Greatest Free Show on Earth."

All of Louisiana's distinct cultures—Native Americans, African Americans, Cajuns, and others—participate in the festivities. The festival developed in Catholic cultures. Mardi Gras means "Fat Tuesday" in French, so named because it begins on the Tuesday before Lent, a time of fasting, and is a traditional time of feasting. Revelers in masks and costumes watch parades of decorated floats wind through the streets. They run to catch fake gold coins, beads, and other trinkets thrown by fully costumed members of krewes (secret organizations), who sponsor the parades. "Throw me some-thin', mista" is a familiar cry.

"Mardi Gras is one big party," one resident of the Big Easy remarks, "and the whole world is invited."

uptown along St. Charles Avenue. The trolley passes by the Garden District, a residential area of antebellum mansions and landscaped gardens—you might even want to hop off and take a walking tour. It is in this quaint section of town that novelist Anne Rice resides. Appropriately enough for someone who writes about vampires and witches, she lives across the street from one of the city's cemeteries. Magazine Street forms the lower border of the Garden District and is a treasure trove of bargain antique shops and boutiques.

Farther uptown, two of the city's major universities—Loyola and Tulane—face tree-lined St. Charles Avenue. You'll find the Audubon Park and Zoological Gardens—perhaps the finest zoo in the South—just across the street from Tulane. An award-winning Louisiana Swamp exhibit features not only alligators and other creatures of the marsh, but also authentic Cajun architecture and food. Rhinos, black bears, cheetahs, and an exotic white tiger named Suri are just a few of the zoo residents.

Why not combine your trip to the zoo with a visit to the Aquarium of the Americas and its more than six thousand specimens of marine life? After your tour, you really should treat yourself to a meal in one of the nearby French Quarter's fine restaurants.

## DOWN ON THE BAYOU IN CAJUN COUNTRY

The Audubon Zoo may give you a glimpse of Louisiana wildlife, but you can see the real thing just a few miles away in Cajun Country. If you take one of the many "swamp tours," you'll get to see snowy egrets, blue herons, alligators, and turtles in their natural habitat.

*"I had the best time on the swamp tour" ten-year-old Chicagoan Tommy Roth exclaims about his trip through the Atchafalaya Swamp. "I saw alligators and herons and snakes. It was cool!"*

But Cajun Country is more than natural beauty. It consists of twenty parishes, each made up of tiny towns, thriving cities, and distinct communities. The commercial center of Cajun Country is Lafayette, the fourth largest city in the state. Almost one hundred thousand people call Lafayette home. Many of them work in the petrochemical industries. The University of Southwestern Louisiana is located here, along with several fine museums that highlight Cajun history and culture. The Acadian Village is a restored bayou town that depicts early nineteenth-century Cajun life, and the Jean Lafitte Heritage and Culture Museum offers exhibits detailing various aspects of Cajun culture.

If Lafayette is the commercial center of Cajun Country, its spiritual heart may just be the Bayou Teche. This snakelike body of water meanders through a number of charming historic towns, each with its own square, Catholic church, and cemetery. (Most cemeteries in southern Louisiana are above ground because the water level is so high caskets would eventually float away.)

*The foot-stomping rhythms of Cajun music can still be heard in restaurants and clubs, and at festivals throughout south Louisiana. "Most of us was raised poor and worked hard," Cajun songwriter D. L. Menard told a reporter. "We had to amuse ourselves with things that didn't cost too much, and music was one way of letting loose."*

St. Martinville, founded in 1760, was one of the first villages settled by Acadians along Bayou Teche. Here is the 157-acre Longfellow-Evangeline State Commemorative Area, a park where Creole plantation life of the mid-nineteenth century is reenacted.

South of Lafayette is another bayou, one that runs south all the way to the Gulf of Mexico. Called Bayou Lafourche and nicknamed "the Longest Main Street in America," it flows for ninety miles through some of the world's richest stores of sugarcane, shrimp, oysters, and oil. In this part of the state, it's likely you'll hear more French than English spoken, so much so that you might think you're in a foreign country. Colly Charpentier, editor of the Thibodaux *Daily Comet*, remembers a shop owner saying to a tourist in the bayou town of LaFourche, "You aren't from around here. You must be American."

Cajun Country stretches east to west from Lafourche Parish to the Texas border and south to north from the Gulf of Mexico to Evangeline Parish. You could spend several weeks exploring just this part of the state. If you do, though, you'll miss the other unique attractions Louisiana has to offer, including a glimpse into the antebellum (pre-Civil War) South found in Plantation Country.

## PLANTATION COUNTRY

Plantation Country is bounded on one side by the Atchafalaya Basin and on the other by the countryside stretching north from Lake Maurepas. Flowing through its center is the Mississippi River, whose gift of rich delta land helped this region to flourish.

# THE EVANGELINE OAK

*This is the forest primeval. The murmuring pines and the*
*     hemlocks,*
*Bearded with moss, and in garments green, indistinct in the*
*     twilight,*
*Stand like Druids of eld, with voices sad and prophetic, . . .*

Alongside the Bayou Teche in one of the oldest towns in Louisiana, St. Martinville, stands the Evangeline Oak. Made famous by Henry Wadsworth Longfellow in his poem called *Evangeline: A Tale of Acadie,* this massive tree is a symbol of the Acadian heritage in the United States. In the poem, a young Acadian woman named Evangeline waits under the tree in vain for her lover, who has married another and will never come. Evangeline's story symbolizes the patience and loyalty of the Acadian spirit. Its penultimate stanza ends with these plaintive words:

*Thousands of throbbing*
*     hearts, where theirs are*
*     at rest and forever,*
*Thousands of aching brains,*
*     where theirs no longer*
*     are busy,*
*Thousands of toiling hands,*
*     where theirs have ceased*
*     from their labors,*
*Thousands of weary feet,*
*     where theirs have*
*     completed their journey!*

Baton Rouge, which became the permanent state capital in 1882, is the economic and cultural center of Plantation Country. Thousands of government workers live in Baton Rouge and its suburbs. Many come to work in the state capitol, the tallest in the country, built by Governor Huey Long. "I can't tell you how many people come in here asking to see the spot where Governor Long was shot," remarks a tour guide. "It is pretty exciting when you think about it."

The view from the capitol's observation deck is extraordinary. You can see huge tankers and other commercial vessels chugging along the Mississippi, living proof that Baton Rouge is the nation's fourth largest port. If you look carefully, you might be able to locate the three-hundred-acre, tree-lined campus of Louisiana State University (LSU). More than twenty-six thousand students study here in Baton Rouge, and several thousand more at university branches in Alexandria, New Orleans, and Shreveport.

Your view from above Baton Rouge will no doubt inspire you to explore the lush countryside that surrounds the capital city. To the east lie the Florida parishes filled with antebellum homes and working farms. In the center of this region, you will find St. Francisville, one of the oldest and still most charming towns in Louisiana.

To the west of Baton Rouge lies the River Road. Lined with elegant plantation homes on one side and oil and gas rigs on the other, the River Road runs south from Baton Rouge almost to New Orleans. On the way, you may want to stop and visit Destrehan Plantation, the oldest documented plantation house in the lower Mississippi Valley.

*Oak Valley plantation in Vacherie seems to whisper of another time, when life was filled with ease and grace in the antebellum South.*

By the time you finish your tour of Plantation Country, you might be ready for a more rugged landscape. For that, you can travel north of Baton Rouge into a region called the Crossroads.

## THE CROSSROADS

Nowhere is the variety of Louisiana landscape more evident than in the central part of the state. Here you'll find hills and prairies, bayous and rich delta land, tiny villages and bustling cities.

At the geographical center of Louisiana lies the city of Alexandria.

Located on the banks of the Red River, Alexandria is a commercial and shipping center with a population of more than fifty thousand people. It is home to the England Air Force Base and other federal military operations, as well as to a branch of Louisiana State University.

Lumber and paper products from surrounding areas come to Alexandria to be shipped to New Orleans and elsewhere. As you travel around the Crossroads, you'll see some of the pine, oak, and cypress forests upon which Louisiana's forestry industry is built. Farmers also grow cotton, sugarcane, and other crops in the lush farmland of the Red River delta.

Winn Parish, located deep in the piney hills northwest of Alexandria, is famous for producing three Louisiana governors: Huey Long, his brother Earl, and O. K. Allen. Farther west, the citizens of Natchitoches proclaim, "We've got more history than anyone else in the state." Since it was the very first settlement in Louisiana and has developed into a modern community of seventeen thousand people, they may be right. The Kisatchie National Forest, a six-thousand-acre forest of hardwood and cypress trees, begins here in the Crossroads and stretches into the northern part of the state. Near Alexandria, the thirty-one-mile Wild Azalea National Recreation Trail offers extravagant floral displays in summer and fall. You can take a canoe ride through the six-mile-long Kitsatchie Bayou or hike through the Kisatchie Hills Wilderness Area. Also known as "Louisiana's Little Grand Canyon," this is an area of mesas, cliffs, and canyons.

If you've made it this far north, though, you've left the Crossroads and entered Sportsman's Paradise.

# PLACES TO SEE

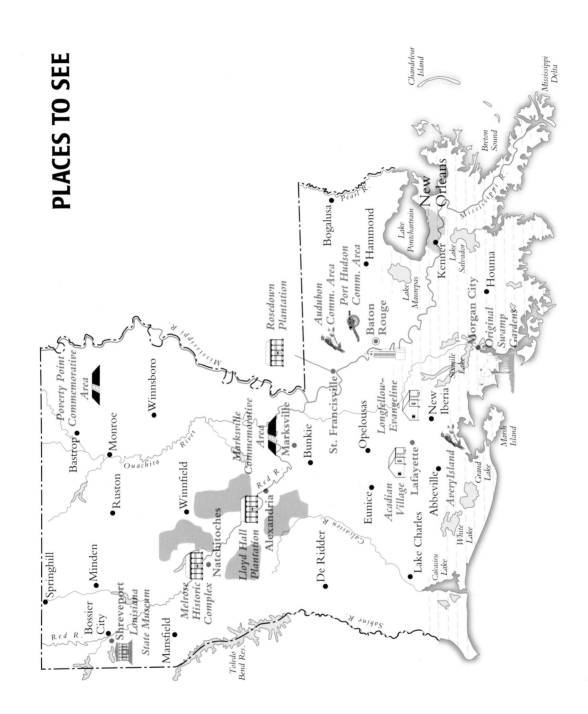

Springhill

Minden

Bossier City

Shreveport

Louisiana State Museum

Mansfield

Red R.

Toledo Bend Res.

Sabine R.

De Ridder

Lake Charles

Calcasieu Lake

White Lake

Grand Lake

Marsh Island

Abbeville

Eunice

Lafayette

Acadian Village

Averylsland

New Iberia

Longfellow-Evangeline

Opelousas

Bunkie

Marksville

Marksville Commemorative Area

Red R.

Alexandria

Lloyd Hall Plantation

Natchitoches

Melrose Historic Complex

Winnfield

Calcasieu R.

Ruston

Monroe

Ouachita River

Bastrop

Poverty Point Commemorative Area

Winnsboro

Mississippi R.

St. Francisville

Rosedown Plantation

Baton Rouge

Port Hudson Comm. Area

Audubon Comm. Area

Bogalusa

Pearl R.

Hammond

Lake Maurepas

Lake Pontchartrain

Lake Salvador

Kenner

New Orleans

Mississippi R.

Breton Sound

Chandeleur Island

Mississippi Delta

Morgan City

Houma

Original Swamp Gardens

Spanish Lake

## SPORTSMAN'S PARADISE

Although this part of Louisiana has its share of bayous and plantation homes, Sportsman's Paradise feels more like the Wild West than the elegant South. This is especially true in the northwestern cities of Shreveport and Bossier City. These twin cities now serve as a center for the sprawling region known as Ar-La-Tex. Ar-La-Tex is a blend of communities in southern Arkansas, northern Louisiana, and eastern Texas. You're just as likely to see advertisements for western-style rodeos and Tex-Mex restaurants as for Dixieland jazz concerts or Cajun cooking here. Horse racing at Louisiana Downs in Bossier City attracts thousands of fans every year.

Traveling east, you'll pass through Claiborne Parish, whose courthouse is one of only four pre-Civil War courthouses still in use. The town of Minden, in Webster Parish, offers a look at the German experience in Louisiana at its Germantown Colony Museum.

No tour of Louisiana would be complete without a visit to the Twin Cities of Monroe and West Monroe. Located on the banks of the scenic Ouachita River, Monroe has a population of nearly fifty-five thousand people, many with jobs in manufacturing and retail trade. The city has much to offer in the way of the arts, including the Strauss Playhouse, an active Opera Club, and the nationally renowned Masur Museum of Art.

If you take the most direct highway routes, you can be back in New Orleans in about four hours. Somehow, though, it's unlikely you will be able to resist taking another look at the many geographical and cultural attractions of the Pelican State on your way back down to the Big Easy.

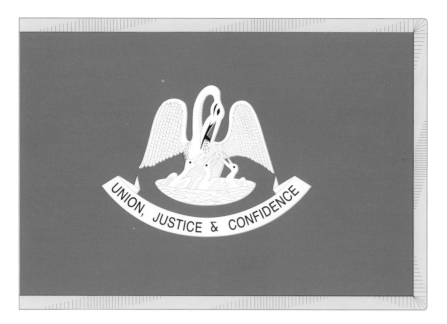

THE FLAG:  The state flag was adopted in 1912 and shows a pelican, the state bird, feeding its young in a nest. Beneath the seal is a white ribbon with the words of the state motto. The background is solid blue.

THE SEAL:  Adopted in 1902, the state seal shows a pelican at the center, tearing flesh from her own breast to feed her young in the nest - a symbol of Louisiana's caring for its people. The state motto encircles the birds, and the words **State of Louisiana** surround the circle.

# STATE SURVEY

**Statehood:** April 30, 1812

**Origin of Name:** Louisiana was named in 1682 for the French king Louis XIV by the explorer René-Robert Cavelier, sieur de La Salle, when he claimed the region for France.

**Nickname:** Pelican State, Bayou State, Creole State

**Capital:** Baton Rouge

**Motto:** Union, Justice and Confidence

**Animal:** Calahoula leopard dog

**Bird:** Brown pelican

**Flower:** Magnolia

**Tree:** Bald cypress

**Gem:** Agate

**Insect:** Honeybee

**Crustacean:** Crawfish

**Fossil:** Petrified palmwood

*Brown pelican*

*Magnolia*

# GIVE ME LOUISIANA

In 1970 the State Legislature adopted "Give Me Louisiana" as the official state song in place of an earlier composition entitled "Song of Louisiana." Then in 1977, yet another song was given official status as an equal partner to "Give Me Louisiana": "You Are My Sunshine," written by ex-Governor Jimmie Davis.

**Words and Music by Doralice Fontane**

# GEOGRAPHY

**Highest Point:** 535 feet above sea level, at Driskill Mountain

**Lowest Point:** 5 feet below sea level, in New Orleans

**Area:** 51,843 square miles

**Greatest Distance, North to South:** 283 miles

**Greatest Distance, East to West:** 315 miles

**Bordering States:** Arkansas to the north, Mississippi to the east, Texas to the west. The Gulf of Mexico lies to the south.

**Hottest Recorded Temperature:** 114° F at Plain Dealing on August 10, 1936

**Coldest Recorded Temperature:** −16° F at Minden on February 13, 1899

**Average Annual Precipitation:** 56 inches

**Major Rivers:** Atchafalaya, Black, Calcasieu, Mississippi, Ouachita, Pearl, Red

**Major Lakes:** Bistineau, Black, Borgne, Caddo, Calcasieu, Grand, Maurepas, Pontchartrain, Sabine, Salvador, White

**Trees:** bald cypress, beech, black walnut, hickory, longleaf pine, magnolia, overcup oak, pawpaw, sassafras, shortleaf pine, sweet gum, tupelo

**Wild Plants:** azalea, camellia, golden club, hibiscus, honeysuckle, iris, jasmine, lily, lotus, marsh hay, milkweed, orchid, pickerelweed, Spanish moss, wild rice

*Alligator*

**Animals:** alligator, beaver, black bear, bobcat, dolphin, diamondback terrapin, Florida panther, gray fox, gray wolf, green water snake, manatee, mink, muskrat, nutria, opossum, raccoon, river otter, sea turtle, skunk, squirrel, sperm whale, weasel, white-tailed deer, wild hog

**Birds:** bald eagle, brown pelican, dove, egret, goose, gull, heron, mallard duck, Mississippi kite, peregrine falcon, pintail duck, quail, red-cockaded woodpecker, teal duck, tern, whooping crane, wild turkey, woodcock

**Fish:** bass, bluefish, bream, catfish, crappie, crawfish, flounder, grouper, oyster, perch, pompano, redfish, shrimp, Spanish mackerel, sturgeon

**Endangered Animals:** Alabama shad, bald eagle, black bear, brown pelican, eastern spotted skunk, Florida panther, green sea turtle, interior least tern, loggerhead sea turtle, manatee, pallid sturgeon, rainbow darter, red-cockaded woodpecker, red wolf, sperm whale, striped dolphin, whooping crane

**Endangered Plants:** bog moss, false foxglove, golden aster, ground plum, hybrid spikegrass, log fern, Louisiana quillwort, slender heliotrope, staghorn clubmoss, swamp thistle, tall bellflower, Virginia anemone, white trout-lily, wild hyacinth

## TIMELINE

**Louisiana History**

c. **300** B.C. Native Americans live in northeastern Louisiana and build huge burial mounds

A.D. 500 Caddos build large villages and ceremonial centers with temple mounds in northern Louisiana

1541 Hernando de Soto discovers the Mississippi River

1682 René-Robert Cavelier, sieur de La Salle, claims the region watered by the Mississippi for France

1699 Louisiana becomes a royal French colony

1714 Natchitoches, first permanent settlement, founded

1718 New Orleans founded and named for Phillippe, duc d'Orléans

1719 First large importation of African slaves

1751 Jesuit priests introduce sugarcane

1762 France cedes Louisiana to Spain

1763 Acadians begin arriving from Canada

1775–1783 American Revolution

1788 Much of New Orleans destroyed by fire

1800 Spain cedes Louisiana back to France

1803 United States purchases Louisiana from France

1812 Louisiana admitted to the Union as the eighteenth state

1812–1814 War of 1812 between the United States and Britain

1815 British defeated in the Battle of New Orleans

1838 First Mardi Gras in New Orleans

1854 Yellow fever ravages Louisiana

1861 Louisiana secedes from the Union

1861–1865 United States Civil War

1862 Federal troops capture New Orleans

1868 Louisiana readmitted to the Union

1893 A hurricane devastates Louisiana

1901 Oil discovered in Jefferson Davis Parish

1915 New Orleans music first called "jazz"

1916 Natural gas field discovered near Monroe

1926 Waterways connecting Lake Charles to the Gulf of Mexico open

1928–1932 Huey P. Long Jr. serves as governor of Louisiana. Elected to the U.S. Senate in 1930.

1935 Former governor Huey Long assassinated in Baton Rouge

1948–1952 Earl K. Long serves as governor

1947 First offshore oil well drilled

1956 World's longest overwater highway bridge opens, crossing Lake Pontchartrain

1960 Public school integration begins

1977 Ernest Morial elected as New Orleans' first black mayor

1984 New Orleans hosts Louisiana World Exposition

1987 Cuban refugees seize the federal detention center in Oakdale

1992 Hurricane Andrew causes extensive damage in southern Louisiana

*Sugarcane*

## ECONOMY

**Agricultural Products:** Soybeans, cotton, rice, sugarcane, corn, yams, sorghum, pecans, beef and dairy cattle, hogs, chickens, shrimp, crawfish, catfish

**Manufactured Products:** Petrochemicals, chemicals, transportation equipment, paper products, processed foods, building materials, electrical equipment, metal products, lumber, printed materials

**Business and Trade:** Wholesale and retail sales, finance, insurance, real estate, banking, research, tourism, commercial fishing, shipbuilding, shipping, transportation

## CALENDAR OF CELEBRATIONS

**Mardi Gras** Possibly the best-known festival in the United States is Mardi Gras. Beginning in January or February, New Orleans celebrates carnival with food and fun for weeks before the 40 days of Lent begin on "Fat Tuesday," *Mardi Gras* in French. Extravagant parades feature floats, marching bands, and masqueraders in flamboyant costumes. Balls are held throughout the city.

**Festival International de Louisiana** In mid-April, Lafayette is host to hundreds of artists from around the world who gather to celebrate the performing and visual arts as well as to enjoy Louisiana's cuisine.

**Crawfish Festival** On the first weekend in May, Breaux Bridge celebrates its fame as "Crawfish Capital of the World" with one of Louisiana's largest festivals. Cajun food, dances, music, folklore, crafts, and contests, including a crawfish race, draw thousands each year.

**Contraband Days** For two weeks in early May, Lake Charles celebrates the role of the pirate Jean Lafitte in Louisiana's history. Festivities include boat races, concerts, arts and crafts, and midway entertainment.

**"Le Cajun" Music Awards Ceremony and Festival** Held in August in Lafayette, the festival features Cajun music, crafts, and food and culminates in the Cajun French Music Association's "Le Cajun" Music Awards.

*Le Cajun Music Festival, Lafayette*

**Louisiana Shrimp and Petroleum Festival** Every Labor Day weekend in September, Morgan City hosts Louisiana's oldest chartered harvest celebration. Festivities include a parade, music, amusement rides, a hands-on children's village, storytelling, and fireworks. A special feature is the blessing of the shrimp boats and the ships that transport Louisiana's oil.

**Louisiana Sugarcane Festival and Fair** On the last weekend in September, New Iberia celebrates one of Louisiana's major products with an agricultural show, displays of quilts, parades, and music. A sugar cookery competition is featured as well as a coronation and ball.

**River City Blues Festival** Baton Rouge honors Louisiana's musical heritage for three days in October with a festival of blues, Cajun, zydeco, and gospel music along with plenty of traditional Louisiana cuisine.

**State Fair of Louisiana** Shreveport is home to the State Fair, one of the largest in the country. The October fair features amusements, food, music, agricultural exhibits, and livestock competitions.

**Christmas Festival of Lights** Louisiana's oldest permanent city, Natchitoches, welcomes the Christmas season on the first Saturday in December with a brilliant festival of lights. Some 140,000 lights are turned on and displayed throughout the city for the entire month.

## STATE STARS

**Louis "Satchmo" Armstrong** (1900?–1971), trumpeter and singer, was born in New Orleans. He first learned music in a boys' home and then with the King Oliver Creole Jazz Band in Chicago. Armstrong developed a distinctive singing and playing style that made him a headliner on tours around the world and earned him the nickname "Satchmo" for his satchel-sized mouth. Armstrong is considered by musicians to be one of the all-time great jazz musicians.

**Truman Capote** (1924–1984), born in New Orleans, gave up formal schooling at the age of 17 and settled in New York City to begin his writing career. His first novel, *Other Voices, Other Rooms*, appeared in 1948 and made him an instant success. Capote continued his career, publishing short stories and novels, including *The Grass Harp* and *Breakfast at Tiffany's*. In 1967, Capote was acclaimed for his book *In Cold Blood*, in which he combined his talents as a novelist and reporter to tell the story of a mass murder in Kansas. Many of Capote's works were adapted for films, television, and the stage.

**Marie Thérèse Coincoin** (1742–1816?) was born a slave, probably near Natchitoches. As a young woman, she lived with a French planter who in 1778 bought her freedom and eventually gave her a large amount of land. Coincoin worked the land, cultivating fields of corn, tobacco, and cotton and raising cattle. She trapped bears and exported their grease as far as Europe. With the profits from her land, she bought the freedom of all her children. After her death, the land was divided among them.

**Harry Connick Jr.** (1967–     ), born in New Orleans, showed exceptional musical talent at an early age. He played the piano in the annual New Orleans Jazz and Heritage Festival from the time he was eight, and as a teenager played in jazz bands in New Orleans clubs. Moving to New York City, Connick launched a singing career. He was heard on the soundtrack of the film *When Harry Met Sally* in 1989. The recording was one of the few jazz releases to be among the top ten on the pop charts. In 1990, Connick won a Grammy Award for the best male jazz vocal performance.

*Harry Connick Jr.*

**Antoine "Fats" Domino** (1928–     ), born in New Orleans, learned to play the piano as a child and began playing professionally in 1948. He gained prominence, as well as his nickname, with the 1949 recording "The Fat Man." Domino went on to produce his rhythm and blues sound in the 1950s with such hits as "Ain't That a Shame," "Blueberry Hill," and "I'm Walkin.'" Domino's recording career lasted into the early 1970s when he began touring the night-club circuit both in the United States and abroad.

*Fats Domino*

**Elizabeth Meriwether Gilmer** (1870–1951) was born in Tennessee but made New Orleans her home for most of her life. In 1894, under the pen name Dorothy Dix, Gilmer began writing an advice column in the New Orleans newspaper *Picayune*. For most of the rest of her life, she dispensed advice on love, life, and how to cope to her loyal followers in her column, "Dorothy Dix Talks." It was estimated that she had some 60 million readers around the world.

**Louis Moreau Gottschalk** (1829–1869), pianist and composer, was born in New Orleans. As a young prodigy, he studied the piano and violin, and at the age of 13 toured Europe giving recitals. In the United States, Gottschalk became one of the most successful and prominent concert performers of his time, playing not only the music of European composers but also his own works, including piano pieces, several symphonies, and two operas.

**Shirley Ann Grau** (1929–     ), a native of New Orleans, is a novelist and short-story writer. She first won acclaim for her book *The Black Prince and Other Stories*, published in 1955. Her first novel, *The Hard Blue Sky*, depicts the lives of a community of French-Spanish descendants of early Louisiana pioneers and received mixed reviews. Grau has said that she does not read reviews and that a writer has to go her own way. She went on to write several additional books, including *The House on Coliseum Street, The Condor Passes,* and *The Keepers of the House*, which won the 1965 Pulitzer Prize for Fiction.

**Lillian Hellman** (1907–1984), born in New Orleans, began her writing career as a reporter in New York City in the 1920s. Her first stage success was the 1934 play *The Children's Hour*, which was followed by *Days to Come* and *The Little Foxes*, plus many others. Hellman's plays often reflect her criticism of social and political injustice, such as the anti-Nazi drama *Watch on the Rhine*, which won the Drama Critics Circle Award in 1941. Her autobiographical works include *An Unfinished Woman* and *Pentimento*.

*Lillian Hellman*

**Clementine Hunter** (1886–1988), a folk artist, was born on a plantation near Cloutierville. Around the late 1920s, Hunter began working as a domestic on the Melrose Plantation near Natchitoches. It was there she developed her artistic talent, painting scenes of everyday life as well as animals and pictures with religious themes. Her works were exhibited in the New Orleans Arts and Crafts shows, and she was the first black artist to receive an exhibition at the New Orleans Museum of Art in 1955. During her long lifetime, Hunter's works were shown in galleries around the country, and many are now part of permanent museum collections.

**Mahalia Jackson** (1912–1972) was born in New Orleans and early on developed a love for blues music. At 13, Jackson moved to Chicago,

Illinois, where she sang at churches and began to make recordings of gospel music. In 1947, Jackson's recording of "Move On Up a Little" became the first million-selling gospel record. Her recordings, live concerts, and television performances earned her a reputation as the world's greatest gospel singer. As

*Mahalia Jackson*

an ambassador of music, Jackson toured Europe and sang at the White House as well as at Martin Luther King Jr.'s March on Washington in 1963. When she died in January 1972, 45,000 people gathered at her funeral to honor her.

**Jean Lafitte** (1770s?–1820s?) was born in France, but little is known of his early life there. Around 1810, he was in Louisiana leading a band of smugglers who operated from the islands in Barataria Bay. Lafitte and his buccaneers sold their smuggled goods and slaves to merchants and planters. Lafitte achieved fame when he aided the American cause in the Battle of New Orleans during the War of 1812. Although pardoned for his former criminal acts, he continued to lead bands of privateers and was famous as a pirate in the Caribbean for several years until he disappeared about 1825.

*Huddie Ledbetter*

**Huddie Ledbetter** (1888-1949), better known as Leadbelly, was a composer and singer born in Morringsport. Leadbelly was a leading figure in the revival of folk music in America and Europe. He was raised in rough conditions in Texas. He spent many years in prison for murder, attempted murder, and assault. While in prison, folklorist Alan Lomax discovered him and recorded his music for the Library of Congress in the 1940s. Two of his most popular songs are "On Top of Old Smokey" and "Good Night Irene."

**Jean-Baptiste Le Moyne, sieur de Bienville** (1680–1768), explorer, colonial official, and founder of New Orleans, was born in Montreal, Canada. He explored the Mississippi and Red Rivers and helped establish colonies at Biloxi, Mississippi, and on Mobile Bay. While serving as governor of France's Louisiana colony, he selected a site for a new settlement on the east bank of the Mississippi River in 1718 and named it La Nouvelle Orléans in honor of France's regent, the duc d'Orléans.

*Elmore Leonard*

**Elmore Leonard** (1925–    ), writer of Westerns and mysteries, was born in New Orleans. He wrote for many years—short stories, novels, and screenplays—until he achieved fame with his suspense stories. Leonard's books are not just thrillers but realistic crime novels with believable people, many of them living on the fringes of society. His first novel, *The Big Bounce*, published in 1969, was followed by works that include *Stick, Glitz, Get Shorty*, and *Pronto*.

**Huey Pierce Long** (1893–1935), governor of Louisiana and U.S. Senator, was born in Winn Parish. Long was a Populist politician who championed the cause of the poor. As governor he promoted social welfare and public projects, while he retained nearly complete control over the state government through patronage. Although he attacked big business for its greed, Long was accused of enriching himself at the public's expense. As a senator, his Share the Wealth plan made him a national figure. In 1935, Long was preparing to challenge the re-election of President Roosevelt when he was assassinated in the Capitol in Baton Rouge.

**Wynton Marsalis** (1961–    ), trumpeter, bandleader, and co-founder of New York City's Lincoln Center Jazz Ensemble, was born in New Orleans into the well-known musical Marsalis family. Trained in both classical music and jazz, Marsalis has toured in the United States and abroad. In 1984, he was the first instrumentalist to win Grammy Awards as both a jazz performer and a classical soloist. Marsalis has composed music for films and ballet and has appeared on television as a spokesperson for the rich tradition of jazz.

*Jelly Roll Morton*

**Ferdinand "Jelly Roll" Morton** (1890–1941), born in New Orleans, was a jazz pianist and composer who began playing the piano in his teens. In 1923, Morton settled in Chicago. Under the name Jelly Roll Morton and His Red Hot Peppers, he recorded his own jazz piano compositions and arrangements. Morton's career as a recording artist was at its height in the 1920s, but his music became less popular in the 1930s when big bands and swing music became the rage. Morton is considered one of the first great jazz composers, but he did not receive widespread recognition until after his death, when interest in traditional jazz was revived.

**Camille Nickerson** (1888–1982), born in New Orleans, devoted her life to the arranging, collection, and preservation of the Creole music of her ancestors. An accomplished musician, Nickerson also toured widely under her stage name "The Louisiana Lady," performing Creole music in concert. She gave up her concert career in the 1920s to teach at Howard University in Washington, D.C., where she continued to research and promote Creole folk music.

**Homer Adolph Plessy** ( ?–1925), the plaintiff in the Supreme Court case *Plessy* v. *Ferguson* in 1896, is thought to have been born in New Orleans and to have worked as a carpenter. Plessy became famous when, in 1892, he challenged the Jim Crow laws of Louisiana by sitting in the white section of a railroad train. He was removed and taken to jail in New Orleans. Backed by a black citizens' group, Plessy appealed to the Supreme Court. The Court declared against Plessy, ruling that segregation in public facilities was legal, a decision that was not overturned until 1954.

**Paul Prudhomme** (1940– ) was born on a farm near Opelousas in the Acadian country. He began cooking with his mother at the age of 7. At 17 he set out to become a cook, working in restaurants around the country for 12 years to learn culinary techniques. He returned to Louisiana, and in 1979 opened his K-Paul's Louisiana Kitchen in New Orleans, which features traditional Creole and Cajun cooking as well as Prudhomme's own unique creations. He is the author of several cookbooks, has been featured on television cooking programs, and in 1980 was the first American chef to receive France's *Merite Agricole* Award.

**Norbert Rillieux** (1806–1894) was born in New Orleans. His father was a wealthy plantation owner; his mother was a slave. Educated in Paris as an engineer, where he also taught, Rillieux returned to Louisiana and began working for a sugar refinery. In 1845, he invented an evaporating system for refining sugar that produced more sugar and greatly reduced the cost of production. Rillieux's system is still used in the refining of sugar.

**Corinne Boggs "Cokie" Roberts** (1943– ), reporter, news analyst, and commentator, was born in New Orleans. Roberts' journalistic career includes work as a reporter for radio stations in New York City and Los Angeles as well as CBS news in Athens, Greece. She also served as a correspondent for National Public Radio and is a regular interviewer and commentator on the television program *This Week with David Brinkley*. Roberts has won the Broadcast Award of the National Organization of Working Women and the Broadcast Award of the National Women's Political Caucus.

**William "Bill" Russell** (1934–   ) was born in Monroe and later moved to Oakland, California. As a college sophomore, Russell became one of the best-known basketball players on the West Coast. In 1957, Russell joined the Boston Celtics, where his talents as a defensive player helped the Celtics win the world championship eight years in a row. Before becoming the Celtics' player/coach in 1966, Russell was named the NBA's Most Valuable Player five times. In 1974, Russell was inducted into the Basketball Hall of Fame.

**Edward Douglass White** (1845–1921), the only justice from Louisiana appointed to the Supreme Court, was born in Lafourche Parish. White served in the Confederate Army during the Civil War and began his political career in Louisiana's state senate. He was later elected to the United States Senate, where he staunchly supported states' rights. In 1894, White was appointed associate justice of the Supreme Court, and in 1910 he was appointed Chief Justice, a position he held until his death. One of White's major contributions on the court was his decision to strike down a discriminatory law that prevented blacks from voting.

*Edward Douglas White*

## TOUR THE STATE

**Poverty Point State Commemorative Area** (Epps) This prehistoric site is a complex of ancient Indian ceremonial mounds dating from 2500 B.C. Early people moved thousands of tons of earth by hand to create the mounds.

**Louisiana State Exhibit Museum** (Shreveport) Dioramas and murals depict Louisiana's prehistory as well as the state's many resources.

**Melrose Historic Complex** (Natchitoches) Melrose is the estate first created by Marie Thérèse Coincoin. There are eight restored buildings, including the Yucca House, made of river-bottom mud and Spanish moss; the African House, built to resemble a house in Africa; and the main mansion.

**Loyd Hall Plantation** (Alexandria) This pre-Civil War estate is the center of a working cotton plantation. Visitors can search for bullet holes and arrowheads and possibly hear some ghosts playing violins.

**Marksville State Commemortive Area** (Marksville) This area is the site of an Indian culture, including earthen mounds, dating from 1400 A.D. A museum specializes in Indian artifacts and exhibits interpreting the culture.

**Acadian Village** (Lafayette) A restored nineteenth-century village features Acadian architecture with homes, a general store, and a chapel. Acadian crafts are also displayed.

**Rosedown Plantation** (St. Francisville) Rosedown, with its 28 acres of historic gardens and moss-draped live oaks, is a pre-Civil War estate where visitors can view the restored contents of the mansion.

**Audubon State Commemorative Area** (St. Francisville) The park includes the old English town of St. Francisville and features Oakley Plantation House, where John James Audubon painted most of his Birds of America series, as well as a bird sanctuary.

**Port Hudson State Commemorative Area** (Port Hudson) Included here is part of the battlefield where the siege of Port Hudson occurred during the Civil War—the first major battle in which African-American Union troops participated. Civil War guns, trenches, and battle re-enactments are featured.

**State Capitol** (Baton Rouge) The site of Huey Long's assassination, the 450-foot-high capitol was built by Long. Constructed of more than 30 kinds of marble, it is the tallest capitol building in the United States.

**Rivertown U.S.A.** (Kenner) A historical district in a Victorian setting, Rivertown features a living-science center, a Louisiana wildlife museum, a Mardi Gras museum, a toy train museum, and a children's castle.

**Louisiana State Museum** (New Orleans) This museum comprises several landmark buildings, including the Cabildo, where the transfer of Louisiana from France to the United States took place. Exhibits here trace Louisiana's history from exploration through Reconstruction. The Presbytère, originally built as a home for priests, displays exhibits on

*Burnside Houmas House*

Louisiana's cultural history. The Old U.S. Mint, an 1835 landmark building, houses exhibits on jazz and Mardi Gras. The 1850 House, an early apartment building, contains furnishings and artifacts depicting Creole lifestyle in the nineteenth century.

**Aquarium of the Americas** (New Orleans) With four major aquatic habitats, including a Caribbean reef, the aquarium is home to more than 7,500 marine creatures and one of the world's largest shark collections.

**Audubon Zoological Gardens** (New Orleans) More than 1,500 animal species are housed in their natural habitats in the zoo, including white alligators in a swamp exhibit.

**Musée Conti Historical Wax Museum** (New Orleans) Visitors learn the story of New Orleans as they view wax figures that include Napoleon Bonaparte, Jean Lafitte, Andrew Jackson, and Louis Armstrong.

**Confederate Museum** (New Orleans) Louisiana's oldest museum exhibits uniforms, weapons, paintings, flags, and other artifacts of the Civil War.

**Garden District** (New Orleans) This district contains elegant mansions built in the 1850s by wealthy business people who did not want to live in the crowded French Quarter.

**Grand Isle** (an island south of New Orleans) Located at the entrance to Barataria Bay, this fishing village is home to a few descendants of the crews of Jean Lafitte's pirate band.

**Jungle Gardens** (Avery Island) Not really an island, this site covers an old salt mine. The gardens abound with all kinds of tropical flowers. A bird sanctuary draws great flocks of egrets, herons, ducks, and other wild birds.

*Atchafalaya Swamp*

**Original Swamp Gardens** (Morgan City) Visitors tour 3-1/2 acres of swamp-land that depicts the habitat and animals in the Atchafalaya Swamp.

**Conrad Rice Mill** (New Iberia) Visitors can tour the oldest rice mill in the United States, which includes a replica of the original company store and displays of Cajun crafts and Cajun folklore.

**Longfellow-Evangeline State Commemorative Area** (St. Martinville) Said to be the locale of Longfellow's poem "Evangeline," this site features the Evangeline Monument as well as the "Evangeline Oak," where visitors can gather to listen to storytellers and hear music. An Evangeline museum features mementos of the Acadian people who settled here.

## FUN FACTS

When Andy Bowen and Jack Burke battled in the boxing ring in New Orleans in April 1893, they made history. Their fight lasted 7 hours and 19 minutes and went 110 rounds. It was the world's longest boxing match, and it ended in a draw.

Although the term "Dixie" to describe the South is thought to be derived from the Mason-Dixon Line, it could be from the French word dix—meaning "ten," which appeared on Louisiana banknotes.

Chef Paul Prudhomme made blackened redfish so famous and popular that a ban was put on catching and serving the fish. Prudhomme and other chefs had to turn to blackened yellowfin tuna.

Cajun dancing is sometimes called "chank-a-chanking" because of the sound made by the little iron triangle that is part of a traditional Cajun band, along with a fiddle and an accordion.

The first Tarzan movie, made in 1917, was filmed in Louisiana.

To help increase its population in the 1700s, the colony of Louisiana encouraged young women in France to emigrate. The women were recruited from orphanages or from "poor but respectable" families. Called Casket Girls because they brought their belongings in a "casket," or chest, they were watched over by the nuns of the Ursuline Convent in New Orleans. One of the nuns' tasks was to help the girls find husbands.

New Orleans' Metairie Cemetery boasts a 60-foot high monument to the memory of Mary Moriarty. It is said that her husband, an Irish immigrant, built the monument so that the people who had snubbed his wife in life would have to look up to her in death.

# FIND OUT MORE

There's lots more to learn about Louisiana! If you'd like to further explore the Pelican State, look in your school library, local library, bookstore, or video store. Here are a few titles to ask for:

## GENERAL STATE BOOKS

Calhoun, Milburn, editor. *Louisiana Almanac: 1995–1996.* Gretna, Louisiana: Pelican Publishing Company, 1995.

LaDoux, Rita C. *Louisiana.* Minneapolis, Minnesota: Lerner, 1993.

Thompson, Kathleen. *Portrait of America: Louisiana.* Milwaukee, Wisconsin: Raintree, 1986.

## SPECIAL LOUISIANA INTEREST BOOKS

Amoss, Berthe. *The Cajun Gingerbread Boy.* New York: Hyperion Books, 1994.

Coil, Suzanne M. *Mardi Gras!* New York: Macmillan Publishing Co., 1994.

Coles, Robert. *The Story of Ruby Bridges.* New York: Scholastic, 1995.

Folse, Pamela. *A Sweet Surprise.* Thibodaux, Louisiana: Blue Heron Press, 1995.

Folse, Pamela. *Bonfire Christmas: A Cajun Holiday Tradition*. Thibodaux, Louisiana: Blue Heron Press, 1994.

Fontenot, Mary Alice. *Mardi Gras in the Country*. Gretna, Louisiana: Pelican Publishing Company, 1995.

Italia, Bob. *The New Orleans Saints*. Minneapolis, Minnesota: Abdo and Daughters, 1995.

Moore, Elizabeth. *Louisiana Indian Tales*. Gretna, Louisiana: Pelican Publishing Company, 1996.

Pisano, Mary Beth. *Going to New Orleans to Visit Weezie Anna: A Child's Eye View of the Unique Phrases and Places of the Crescent City*. Brandon, Mississippi: Quail Ridge Press, 1994.

Thomassie, Tynia. *Feliciana Feydra LeRoux*. Boston: Little, Brown and Company, 1995.

Vidrine, Beverly B. *A Mardi Gras Dictionary*. Lafayette, Louisiana: Sunflower Press, 1994.

## VIDEOTAPES

"Audubon: New Orleans' New Zoo." Cut Off, Louisiana: Cote Blanche Productions, 1987.

"Gumbo Goes Downtown." Shawnee Mission, Kansas: Marsh Media, 1993.

## COMPUTER DISK

"Evangeline: A Study in Cajun Culture." Center for French and Franco-phone Studies (Louisiana State University), Foundation CODIFIL, National Data Products.

# INDEX

Page numbers for illustrations are in boldface.